D1521471

The Other Side

Flourishing In Veteran Life

JASON RONCORONI

All proceeds from this book will be donated to veteran organizations that specialize in supporting military transition.

Dedication to the late Don Ollar was written by his daughter, Katelyn Ollar, with photo provided by his wife, Sue Laird Ollar.

Cover image of the Phoenix was copied from the wikipedia page: https://en.wikipedia.org/wiki/Phoenix_(mythology)#/media/File:Phoenix_(1583).svg, considered public domain with an original copyright of 1583.

The Other Side

DEDICATION

This book is dedicated to the late COL (R) Donovan Ollar, who took his own life in February of 2022. He was not just a husband, and a father, but a soldier through and through. He proudly served for twenty-seven years and eventually seven deployments took their toll. He attended West Point and there he was prepared for a life in the army. What he wasn't prepared for was life after. He had PTSD and like most veterans he preferred to suffer in silence rather than ask for help because it's often associated with weakness. Through that he was still a man who above all else continued to uplift those around him even when he was at his darkest. He was ready for the change in job and atmosphere but the military didn't prepare him for the loss of camaraderie in the civilian world. His job no longer had the level of responsibility he was used to and he was surrounded by coworkers who he couldn't relate to. To everyone around him he seemed fine, happy even, but you never really know what's going on inside someone else's head.

When we ask someone how they are we don't really want to know the honest answer, we want them to tell us everything is fine and then we feel better about ourselves because we asked them in the first place. At a certain point we can no longer accept that as a valid answer, ask again, make sure they know you genuinely care about their response. When someone asks "How are you doing?" it's hard to answer honestly when you aren't doing well, no one wants to burden loved ones with the demons they're trying so hard to bury. If I take anything away from losing my dad I now see the world from his viewpoint, the little things bring me joy.

Anger I was holding onto feels like a waste of energy because we are not guaranteed tomorrow. In the past whenever I heard the phrase "tomorrow is not promised" I always took it as I was not promised to wake up each morning, it never occurred to me that tomorrow with him wasn't promised. It's easy to get hung up on small slights people have made to you, but when we only focus on how people have hurt or wronged us we overlook all the positives we have in our life. Losing my dad forever changed my life. I honestly believe I will never be whole again, and yet I am so grateful for everything he taught me in the time we did have together. So I ask one thing of you reading this, please check on those you love. Check on your battle buddies, or someone you've been meaning to text or call but never found the time, because before you know it time's run out.

'Til we see you again…Beat Navy!
~ Mama, Bug and Bee

Shelby, Don, Sue and Katelyn Ollar

CONTENTS

CHAPTER 1

MY STORY

*A*t first, I didn't know where I was.

I felt like I had just awoken from a deep sleep. I looked around the room to get my bearings. I was in a hospital bed. I was wearing a gown, and I had a number of wires and tubes emanating from my body. I could hear the beeps and noises from the monitoring devices attached to me. On the opposite side of the room was a television mounted on the wall. It was on, but the sound was muted. I had some cuts and bruises on my arm, but I wasn't in any pain. There was a handwritten note on the service tray in front of me:

YOU ARE OKAY. YOU HAD A HEART ATTACK. YOU ARE IN THE HOSPITAL. YOUR WIFE KNOWS THAT YOU ARE HERE. PUSH THE BUTTON IF YOU NEED ANY ASSISTANCE.

Seriously? A heart attack? No . . . that did NOT happen.

I placed my hand on my chest as if expecting to find some evidence of open heart surgery. Nothing. I could feel my heart beating. Nothing out of the ordinary. For the most part, I felt — normal. I did a quick scan of my body. I noticed some numbness in my left leg, but that could have been from how I was positioned on the bed. A heart attack? I couldn't believe it. It didn't make sense. My attention turned to the note in front of me. How could you write "You are okay" and "You had a heart attack" on the same line? I was confused, and I felt terribly alone.

Was I really awake, or am I still dreaming?

1

THE BEGINNING

*M*y story begins in Coopersburg, a small town about an hour north and west of Philadelphia in southern Pennsylvania. I grew up in a suburb of Allentown — a city made famous for its blue collar culture and the steel industry immortalized in a song by Billy Joel from the early eighties.

My parents came from humble beginnings. They both grew up in poverty. My father was raised in a single-parent household. There were days when he didn't have food to eat and cold nights when he would share a bed with his brother and sister for body warmth because they didn't have any heat. My dad barely graduated from high school, and when he did, he got a job working in a bank — back when you had to physically walk into a bank to do business. He got his accreditations to become a mortgage broker and got involved in business lending.

My mother grew up in the projects of northern New Jersey. Her father built the house she would eventually call home. When she graduated from high school, she went to nursing school — back when that was how you became a registered nurse.

As a kid, my mom worked in the hospital at night, and my dad worked in the bank during the day. What they wanted for their three kids — I have an older sister and a younger brother — was the opportunity to attend college. Like most baby boomers, they wanted their children to have it better than they did, and they believed that a college education was how to ascend from the lower middle class. My mom and dad worked very hard to give us a life they didn't have, but we were not wealthy. We didn't have the money to send three kids to college, so part of my search included scholarships and other options to offset the cost. Attending college from my small part of the universe meant community college or a state school. I didn't want to follow my classmates up to Happy Valley to attend Penn State. I wanted to do something different. I wanted to experience something exciting.

My family didn't have a strong military heritage. My uncle was drafted for Vietnam, but both my grandparents failed their physicals and couldn't serve during World War II. Much of my impression of the military was shaped by those classic eighties movies from my teenage years: *First Blood, Red Dawn, Top Gun, Platoon,* and *Full Metal Jacket* to name a few. When I was a junior in high school, I got invited to attend a recruiting event for West Point. I had no idea what West Point was, but I learned that it was different from what was considered "regular" college. It was also free, so for me, it checked all the right boxes.

This event was off Lehigh Street in downtown Allentown. I went with my dad. I assumed that this was just like any other college fair: I would show up, add my name to the mailing list, ask some questions, grab a brochure, and be on my way. I was wrong.

I walked into a room with arranged seating. There was a projector and screen for a formal presentation. In attendance were representatives from our local congressman's office and even a cadet wearing the traditional white over gray uniform. Everyone else was wearing a shirt and tie, and some even wore suits. Not me. I walked in wearing a Led Zeppelin concert shirt, stone washed jeans, and my Chuck Taylor high tops. I was clueless. This was clearly a world that I knew nothing about.

Once I overcame my initial embarrassment, I sat in my designated seat and listened to their recruiting pitch. They had a video presentation which showed cadets rappelling out of a helicopter, sliding down zip lines high over a lake, and parachuting through the clear blue sky. I was captivated. I didn't fall in love with the army, but I was impressed with how different this was from anything I had expected — and it was paid for. I knew right then and there that I wanted to go to West Point after high school.

Two weeks after graduation and a little more than a month after my eighteenth birthday, I showed up at the Holleder Center and began my journey through the military. I was still clueless. I didn't know what I wanted to study. In a place like West Point, your social circles were shaped by athletic teams or your program of study. I didn't have Division 1 athletic talent, and most of my friends studied engineering. Consequently, I majored in engineering. I was good at math and science, and I figured that an engineering degree from a place like West Point wouldn't hurt me later in life.

As for the army, I didn't really know what I wanted to do. Based on the video I saw during the recruiting event, I knew I wanted to jump out of airplanes and rappel out of helicopters. I also thought it would be exciting to learn how to fly. I went to airborne school during summer training before my junior year, and I followed that up with air assault training during the summer before my senior year. When I graduated with my degree in mechanical engineering, I was commissioned into aviation and went to Fort Rucker, Alabama to learn how to fly. Once I got my wings, I accomplished everything I had wanted to do in the army, so my plan was to leave. I wanted to take my West Point education and try my luck in the corporate world — which is exactly what I did.

I resigned my commission and partnered with a junior officer hiring company to find civilian employment. I went to one of their career conferences, and I crushed it. I had no less than 11 interviews and received six job offers. I accepted a job with Lucent Technologies and returned back to the Allentown area in southeastern Pennsylvania.

I was hired as a manufacturing process engineer, which is a fancy name for the engineering representative on the production floor of a manufacturing facility. Lucent was an optoelectronics company that produced high end, fiber optic communications equipment. I had no idea what our products did, but those details didn't matter. Like Tom Smykowski from the movie *Office Space*, my job was to take the messages from the union supervisors on the production line and share them with the development side of the company and vice versa. I had the "people skills" necessary to bridge the gap between design and manufacturing, and I learned very quickly in that role that I didn't want to be an engineer.

My plan at the time was to take advantage of the company's generous tuition assistance program and get an MBA from nearby Lehigh University. I figured that I would stay in my current role to get some professional experience, and by the time I completed my masters degree, I would find another job — either at Lucent or somewhere else. I thought this was a solid plan.

It was the spring of 2001. I had been working in my current role for nearly eight months, and I completed the first two courses for my MBA. That was when the dot-com bubble burst. When that happened, the entire economy fell into a recession, but for the tech sector, that was a catastrophic event. Lucent had three manufacturing facilities in the region — one in Allentown, one in Breinigsville, and one in Reading. Within three months, all three of those facilities shut down, and they laid off thousands — if not tens of thousands — of employees — including me. All of a sudden, my well laid plan for future employment was no longer viable. I was facing a new crisis of having to secure employment during an economic downturn.

Unfortunately, I didn't know how to find a job. I did whatever the junior officer hiring company told me to do to secure the job at Lucent. I didn't know how to tailor a resume. I had never heard of "networking." I didn't know how to craft a cover letter. Consequently, I did the only thing that I thought I could do. I started to shotgun blast my crappy resume on Monster.com to any and every job that remotely sounded like something I could do. I was applying to at least ten job postings a day for a myriad of positions in the local area.

If you happen to know anything about the hiring process, then you know that how I was doing it is exactly the wrong way to do it. I didn't know any better, and nobody was offering any guidance or assistance. I wasn't getting many responses, and the few I did get were straightforward rejections without any feedback.

It didn't take long for me to run out of money. I was broke. Flat broke. I could not afford my apartment. I couldn't make the payments on my car. I needed a place to live, and I didn't have any good options at the time. I was a 30 year-old man who graduated near the top of his class at West Point, and I had to move back in with my parents. This was a low point in my transition and also in my life.

While I was at mom and dad's house I had an idea. I started to explore the possibility of flying for the Coast Guard. I got a lot of flight time as a junior officer in the army. I also fancied myself as a beach person having spent many summer months as a teenager working at the Jersey Shore. The Coast Guard was different from the army, and perhaps a better fit. If nothing else, it was a job with a decent salary and health benefits that could provide a soft landing or a solid foundation for my next step.

I learned very quickly that when I resigned my commission in the army, I was placed on the Inactive Ready Reserve (IRR). This meant that I couldn't just "sign up" for the Coast Guard because technically, I was still in the army. If I wanted to join the Coast Guard, I had to first get released by the army and do a service transfer to the Coast Guard. In order to do that, I had to complete a bunch of paperwork that required a series of endorsements and recommendations from previous supervisors in the army.

That last part was going to be a problem. I wasn't comfortable reaching out to any of my former bosses because when I was a junior officer, I was kind of a jackass. Let me explain: I was commissioned with the intention of leaving the army as soon as my time was up. I had the immaturity that comes from being a 22 year-old, service academy graduate combined with the arrogance of being a pilot. Additionally (and somewhat ironically), I was fairly competent in my job. In other words, I was good at what I did but had a terrible attitude about how I did it. I had plenty of well-intentioned leaders who encouraged me to grow up and change my attitude. I didn't listen. I thought I was better than the army. In my head, the army was holding me back. I was not just defiant, but I was defiant in a very condescending and offensive way.

Now, here I was a year later — broke and living at home with my parents. I didn't have a job. Hell, I didn't have a lead much less an interview. Things clearly didn't work out the way I thought they would. I had no idea what I wanted to do with my life, but this Coast Guard option was the first thing I had been excited about in some time. Unfortunately, I had no idea how people might respond to me if I reached out for help given how I left.

I felt vulnerable in a very uncomfortable way. I was embarrassed and somewhat ashamed. I'm not sure I could've handled any more rejection at this point in my life, but I figured, what do I have to lose? If people laughed at me or simply ignored my requests, my situation wouldn't get any worse. I saw only upside, so I opened myself up. I crafted a very heartfelt email to four different leaders who I respected deeply at the time. I sent this message out on a Monday with the hope of hearing back by Friday. Fortunately for me, I received four responses the very next day. All of the messages said basically the same thing — they were very sorry that I was in a bad place and they were more than willing to help in any way they could. Apparently, I didn't acknowledge or appreciate the quality of people who were part of my life at the time.

I started to have more meaningful conversations about my life for the first time in my life. When I spoke to one of my mentors on the phone, he made the astute observation that — since the day I joined the army, I had been trying to push it away at every opportunity. He was right. That is exactly what I had done since I reported to the cadet with the red sash on my first day at West Point. On the heels of that observation, he asked me how that approach had been working out for me. Admittedly, this was a tongue in cheek question to which I responded that things were clearly not well. After that, he asked, "If this is what it looks like when you push it away, what would it look like if you embraced it?" It was an intriguing question to be sure, but also one that I was not ready to consider.

You have to remember where my state of mind was at the time. Even as my life had fallen apart, I clung to the idea that I was still better than the army. There was a certain amount of shame that came from the notion that I was failing in the civilian world. Going back to the army would mean getting pushed back to a later cohort year group. All of my friends and fellow classmates would outrank me. Additionally, I wasn't the best steward of my career. I didn't do the right jobs in the right ways to set myself up for promotion because I never planned on staying in the army. This is not to say that I was a promotion risk, but promotion certainly wasn't a guarantee. This didn't seem to be a very enticing course of action for someone who didn't want to be in the army in the first place.

Keep in mind that I was working at a dive bar in downtown Allentown at the time. It was a job that required me to wear a baseball hat and a shirt with a name tag. Most of the people I worked with were much younger than me. When you find yourself in a role like that, you have plenty of time to reflect on your life — especially on the days when you are closing after midnight.

One of the thoughts that haunted me was the idea that I never gave the army a fair chance — not really. When you included my time at West Point, I had given nearly half of my life to the military. I started to think that maybe I owed it to myself to give it an honest shot. That thought was reinforced by the fact that I didn't have any other good options at the time. Even if I went back, the worst that could happen is that I would get passed over for promotion in three years and end up right back here — at the bottom of the barrel of a dead end job. That said — a lot could happen in three years. For all these reasons, I decided to return to the army with the commitment to do it differently this time.

I wrote an email to my mentor to share my intentions. The subject of the message from my Yahoo account was "What to do" and I sent that message at 4:37 pm on the evening of September 10, 2001. The next day, the whole world changed.

I would love to tell people how I was inspired to return to the army in the service of my country during its hour of need, but my story is not the same as Pat Tillman's. The truth is that I had made a number of decisions that simply didn't work out for me, and I saw returning to the army as an opportunity to reboot my career and my life.

That said, when I went back in, I was ALL in. I changed my attitude. I grew up. I walked into a job that nobody wanted because I didn't have much of a choice. I did that job for two and half years, and I completed my first combat deployment to Afghanistan.

After that, I was assigned to Fort Polk, Louisiana. I was an observer controller at the Joint Readiness Training Center (JRTC). This was another job that people didn't want, and I got there right at the time when operations in Afghanistan and Iraq were running on full throttle. At JRTC, our job was to complete the validation training for conventional forces before they deployed into combat. The optempo was ridiculous. For a stateside assignment, we had a brutal schedule. We were working 25 days on, 5 days off, and we completed 22 unit rotations in 24 months.

That job did two things for me. First, it boosted my confidence about how to lead aviation operations in the current conflict, and second, because we worked with just about every unit in the army, I was exposed to every rising leader in the aviation community. I believe that experience combined with the exposure is what ultimately resurrected my career.

My next assignment was to the Command and General Staff College in Fort Leavenworth, Kansas. Once I completed my schooling, I was assigned to the storied 101st Airborne Division in Fort Campbell, Kentucky. While there, I did my second and third year-long deployments to Afghanistan including the surge of combat operations in 2010 with Task Force Destiny. After that, I was assigned to the Joint Staff where I worked in the basement of the Pentagon for two years. Then I was selected to command a general support aviation battalion at Hunter Army Airfield in Savannah, Georgia.

Truth be told, I loved the army, but I always knew that — at some point, I would have to leave again. I had an engineering degree that I didn't want to use. I got another degree in Industrial-Organizational Psychology that I didn't know how to use. Now I had a wife and two kids, and my confidence was waning. I still carried the scars from my first transition from the military.

In an effort to solidify my confidence and marketability, I decided to finish my MBA. I went through the MBA@UNC program at the University of North Carolina. Most of this program was completed online with a series of in-person immersion sessions. The first immersion took place at the main campus in Chapel Hill. One of the focus areas of this event was career development — understanding what you intended to do with your MBA after graduation. In preparation for this weekend experience, I completed a series of assessments and surveys designed to align my interests, skills, and experience with potential career paths. Fortunately for me, graduation from the MBA program coincided with my projected retirement date from the military. This was a great opportunity to get clarity about what I might do once I retired after battalion command.

When I sat down with the career counselor, she handed me a folder with the printouts of my assessments and reports. On the cover was a summary page that ranked possible career fields based on my results. At the top of the list it said "coaching and mentoring." My counselor asked me what I thought about this. I said that coaching and mentoring were simply a part of being a leader in the military. I already knew I enjoyed doing that. I didn't need to fill out this paperwork to figure that out.

As a follow-up, she asked if I had ever considered becoming a professional coach. I said that I simply didn't know enough about football or basketball to be a professional coach. She laughed. She thought I was kidding. I wasn't. I had no idea what she was talking about.

She tried to explain by describing coaching from the perspective of a "life" or a "leadership" coach. At that point, I laughed. I had never heard of such a thing. This sounded like something advertised on late night infomercials for people who couldn't find real jobs. To be honest, I was a bit insulted. I thought her question suggested that my education and experience simply didn't measure up in the civilian world, and this "made up job" was the best I could do. This was my awkward introduction to the profession of coaching.

The counselor told me that the field of consulting had evolved since the turn of the century. Coaching was a real thing that was becoming more popular in the leadership development genre. She did her best to convince me that this was a viable profession, but I wasn't buying it.

Instead, I came up with a different plan. Given my experience as a battalion commander, I thought that if I could find a job that allowed me to do the things I enjoyed from that role, I would be just fine. Through a bit of networking I connected with a national nonprofit organization that focused on the issue of military and veteran suicide. That sounded like a worthwhile cause while working with a very familiar segment of the population.

At the time, I didn't know anything about the nonprofit sector. I thought that nonprofits were charities that solicited donations during the annual Combined Federal Campaign. Despite the nobility of the endeavor, I wasn't confident that this type of employment could provide a sustainable salary. After some research and networking, I was convinced otherwise. I took this job under the assumption that I would be able to do all the things I loved as a battalion commander: create an ambitious vision, build a high performance team, expand our operations, and create and collaborate to address this heart wrenching issue plaguing the veteran community. I was thrilled to take on this role as a continuation of my commitment to service.

Unfortunately, I was completely wrong about the job. At its core, the organization managed a call center. Part one of my job was to manage said call center, and I had no desire to be a call center manager. Part two of the job was business development. I had to represent the organization at conferences, events, and symposiums around the country that addressed suicide awareness, suicide prevention, mental health, and veteran wellness. I didn't mind attending these events, but the travel requirement was significant. Much of it occurred over weekends. I had no desire to be away from my family like that. Part three of the job was to generate revenue. Every business has to make money, but I didn't want to be the guy on the phone asking people for money — especially when it was to do these two other things that I didn't want to do in the first place.

This was the wrong job for me, so I resigned after a

year. In doing so, I found myself in the familiar and unwanted situation of trying to figure out what I wanted to do with my life all over again. If you look at my break in service as a junior officer — which was 19 months — and add that to the first year and a half after my retirement, you get a three-year arc where I had eight different jobs. My strategy for securing employment was clearly not working.

About a month after I quit my job, I had a phone conversation with someone who I had been networking with from my MBA program. She worked in the executive leadership and development field. Her organization was looking to hire a program manager, and she immediately thought of me. Once she confirmed the position, she sent an email asking me to call her as soon as possible. When I did, her enthusiasm was overwhelming. She was excited about the prospect of me joining their team. Admittedly, I also got excited — all the way up to the point when I asked her about the details of the job. The only thing that interested me was the fact that she was so interested in hiring me. My energy level came crashing back down to earth. I realized that I didn't have trouble finding a job. My problem was finding the right one.

Looking back, I was very bitter the first time I left the military. I wanted to prove my worth. I sought a job with an important title that offered more money than I was making as an officer in the army. When I retired, I chose to stay close to the community I had just left. I thought that if I could just do the same kind of work I was doing as a battalion commander, then I would be just fine. In both cases, I found exactly what I was looking for but nothing that I truly wanted. If I kept on doing what I had been doing, I knew I would be miserable for the foreseeable future. In an effort to break this cycle, I decided to do something drastic. I decided to take a leap of faith.

I did a google search for coaching. I had no idea what it was at the time. I found a training program about 30 minutes away from where I lived at the time. This nine month program was beginning in a few weeks, and it was very expensive. I thought that if I could enroll and figure out how to pay for this program, I would do it. I would explore the idea of becoming a coach. At this point, what did I have to lose? This was how my journey into professional coaching began.

My leap of faith paid off. Once I began down a path that aligned with my identity and what I really wanted to do with my life, I started to generate positive momentum. I didn't know how to launch or manage my own business. I did not take a single class about entrepreneurship or small business management when I got my MBA, but I figured it out and have been bouncing against the guard rails along this road since 2017. Along the way, I wrote two bestselling books, and now, I talk to leaders like you about what you want to do in life beyond the military.

Looking back, if you had told me a year before retirement that this is how I'd be living my life, I would have laughed my way out of the room. I never thought my life would pan out this way, and yet here I am. Now that I am here, I couldn't imagine doing anything else. This has been my journey through the military and the return home to civilian society — the ordinary world. I thought that I had finally made it, but on the morning of September 4, 2021, my journey almost ended. Apparently, I still had a long way to go.

CHAPTER 2

THE JOURNEY

"*Y*ou died."

That seemed a bit extreme, but it was how the nurse answered me when I asked about what had happened.

I thought that near death — or actual death — experiences were accompanied by a bright light and visions of past family members welcoming you into the afterlife. I didn't experience any of that. If I did, I didn't remember it. I didn't remember anything. For me, it was as if I had just awoken from a deep sleep — one that lasted two days.

"The kind of heart attack you had is not survivable," she explained. "I've never seen it before. You are lucky to be here."

It was Labor Day weekend. On Saturday morning, I went out for a 7 mile run. Nothing was out of the ordinary. I had no discomfort that I could remember, and I wasn't in any pain at the time of this conversation. I could recall no dizziness or shortness of breath. When I finally had a chance to check my phone several days later, I was able to see exactly where and when I went down. My run ended at 6.83 miles. I was almost finished. I was just about to enter my neighborhood and walk the final half mile to my house. Obviously, I didn't make it.

Paramedics brought me to the hospital. At the time, they didn't know why I had collapsed. I appeared relatively fit for a 50 year old man. I had been running about 20 miles a week before this event. Their initial thought was that my condition was drug related. Heart attack was not a likely diagnosis.

Once I got to the hospital, the cardiologist performed a coronary angioplasty of the left anterior descending artery — otherwise known as the "widow maker" artery due the lethality of blockages that originate from this location. The doctor inserted a stent through a vein in my right leg — which would explain the bandage on my upper thigh. He ordered a number of scans and tests to assess the level of cardiovascular disease in other parts of my body. Luckily, this was the only blockage — a rather unique circumstance for such a catastrophic event.

After my conversation with the nurse, I felt very alone and afraid. I was scared. I had no physical symptoms. If a medical professional hadn't explained it, I wouldn't have believed it. I was in the intensive care unit, and because of COVID protocols, my wife couldn't be there. Jill was able to drop off a handwritten note and one from each of my boys, Aidan and Everett. She also provided a bunch of pictures and some reading material — mostly comic books.

Before she left, the nurse told me how to use the phone to dial out of the hospital.

More than anything else, I really needed to hear my wife's voice.

THE MILITARY ADVENTURE

*M*y generation identifies with a number of movies that describe growing up in the eighties. Perhaps you remember the meaning of the phrase "Save Ferris." Our group of friends included a brain, an athlete, a basket case, a princess, and a criminal who we met during Saturday detention. You recognize that St. Elmo's is a bar in Georgetown even if you've never been to Washington DC.

Wolverines meant more to us than a school mascot, and you know that when Frankie Goes To Hollywood, he doesn't walk the streets of Santa Carla after sunset. If you smile as you read these words, then alas — you are my people! Allow me to share some context about the military adventure from another popular movie from the eighties.

As a teenager, I could identify with Danny LaRusso from *The Karate Kid*. I'm guessing that you could too. Danny, a character played by actor Ralph Macchio, was just an average, insecure kid who overcame the inherent adversity of teenage adolescence to become a champion, the hero who triumphed over the bullies from the Cobra Kai Dojo. It's a feel good story, but who among us didn't desire a chance to conquer the demons of our youth on our way to the top of the winner's platform? The military gave us a chance to do just that. We could be a part of something bigger than ourselves, and in doing so, shed the insecurities of our youth and become something more — our own chance to be a hero. Danny had the perfect ending to his story. Unfortunately, ours is not as clean as a Hollywood production compressed into a 126 minute run time.

Each of us has our reasons for joining the military. For some, it was a chance to pay for college. For others, it satisfied a craving for adventure — leaving the anonymity of our small town, seeing the world, and doing something exciting. After 9/11, that call to service had focus. We had a cause. We had a chance to be part of something historic. We could be the hero. 9/11 was a day that would define the military experience of our entire generation.

Service during a time of war is hard — especially for those who take up the mantle of leadership. Decisions have real consequences on the lives of the men and women with whom we serve. Too often, we have to make less than optimal choices to achieve the mission against the pressure of bringing everyone home safely to their families. This stress begins as a slow simmer in our consciousness that builds into a boil as our deployment date draws near.

Once we arrive in combat, we are tormented by the persistent anxiety that accompanies the uncertainty of war. We are consumed with fear and the possibility of losing anyone. May God help us if we do. The remainder of our lives will forever be haunted by the constant rumination of what we could or should have done differently. We will wonder if their sacrifice was worth the cost. Guilt and regret begin to cast a wide shadow over our mental and emotional well-being. We realize that there are no trophies or winner's podium at the end of this journey. We fade into obscurity with our shame in the darkness. This harsh reality is a far cry from what we once hoped to attain from this adventure.

As difficult as this might be to hear, the darkness is part of the journey. In the words of the samurai warlord Uesugi Kenshin, "Those who cling to life die, and those who defy death, live." What we experience through this exposure to the limits of the human condition — the good, the bad, and the ugly — becomes a part of who we are and the leaders we are meant to become.

The military experience tests the limits of our potential. We can explore how this occurs using the rubric of basic, psychological, and growth needs from Maslow's Hierarchy. Basic needs are addressed through the predictable paycheck and suite of benefits for the service member and their family. In terms of psychological needs, the military provides a strong sense of belonging forged through an honorable group identity. Camaraderie is perhaps the most endearing quality of military service. Additionally, the military's culture validates and reinforces esteem through the recognizable uniforms, customs and courtesies, rank structure, and rituals steeped in tradition. Finally, the nature of the work itself challenges leaders to push beyond the known performance boundaries. We have to. Lives depend on it. The military requires the very best of its people, and therefore pushes each of us to become the very best version of ourselves.

On a hormonal and neurological level, we feel this sense of satisfaction through the steady release of oxytocin, serotonin, dopamine, and endorphins — otherwise known as the "happiness chemicals." The flow of oxytocin is fueled by trusted relationships and love — especially love — that comes from that deep sense of camaraderie. The serotonin is fueled by the esteem that comes from doing meaningful work as part of a respected team. The novelty of achievement through challenging and complex situations provides the high we feel from hits of dopamine. Endorphins allow us to push past the discomfort of the moment to attain the state of flow that enables us to realize the upper limit of our performance potential. The chemical resonance from these hormones and neurotransmitters helps to optimize both performance and subjective well-being despite the inherent danger and difficulty of the job.

The military journey offers each of us a chance to flourish — and truly live. According to renowned psychologist Dr. Martin Seligman, flourishing is a function of five related qualities: positive emotions, engagement, relationships, a deep sense of purpose and meaning, and achievement (also known as the PERMA Model in the parlance of positive psychology). Once you've experienced life at the top of your game, anything less is entirely inadequate. Finding an opportunity that continues growth in life beyond the military is the essential challenge of our transition to a civilian life.

Failure to discover empowering opportunities that build on your experience could lead to a state of languishing and, in some cases, despair. Merely settling for a job that only meets your most basic needs of financial security without addressing your intrinsic drive for individuation could prove extremely hazardous to your psychological well-being. When combined with the residual mental and emotional consequences of military service, the resulting impacts could be devastating. We see the evidence of this across the veteran community through the preponderance of mental health and related issues that include substance abuse, anxiety disorders, depression, and suicide. Navigating the void that exists between life in the military and life beyond the military is the most precarious part of your journey.

This is further complicated by limiting perspectives about the military experience that ignore or marginalize the potential of veteran leaders. One is the idea that leaving the military is somehow the end. It's not. Transition is but one requirement along the path to a higher state of being. According to Joseph Campbell, there are 17 steps to the Hero's Journey, and it doesn't end when you return to the ordinary world. When you consider the anthropological precedent of military transition throughout history, warriors return from the battlefield and ascend into positions of greater responsibility. They become the wise elders, chieftains, and statesmen of the tribe. They are charged with applying the wisdom and experience from the military adventure to improve the overall condition of society.

Society's warriors are meant to lead after they've returned home from the battlefield. They have an obligation to serve a higher purpose, and so were you. Unfortunately, the language around the transition process sets expectations that are much less inspiring. We sign out of the military on "terminal" leave. As mentioned before, separation or retirement is not the end. To say that you are a "Soldier for Life" implies that the warrior identity persists beyond the service. It doesn't. You become something different, and ideally, you become something more. To suggest that you have been "institutionalized" like a prisoner from the penal system hints at an element of criminality in your warrior identity. This association subconsciously reinforces the guilt and shame that accompanies the combat experience. Suggesting that a military commander is unqualified for a commensurate position of leadership in business because it would be inappropriate to place a senior business leader in command completely neglects the unique approach to leader development in the military and its universal application to improved performance outcomes. Leadership is a human quality, and what makes military leaders more capable is the fact that their development occurs at the extremes of the human condition.

Transition is not a mission. Life after the military is not an encore performance. It is the main show. Primitive tribes used elaborate rituals to acknowledge the psychological and spiritual evolution necessary for the warrior to reintegrate back into the tribe. This is not "retirement" in a traditional sense that suggests we are finished working when — anthropologically speaking — our most important work lies ahead. Our modern traditions and retirement ceremonies lack the luster and significance to appropriately acknowledge this transformation. Military transition is meant to be an empowering experience that we frame from an entirely negative and self-limiting point of view. Even worse, we are left to navigate the threshold between these two worlds alone. It's no wonder why so many veterans struggle when they attempt to reintegrate back into society.

We assume that the military was our calling, especially in the wake of 9/11, but it's not. It is the initiation to drive the mental, emotional, and spiritual growth toward self-actualization and ultimately individuation consistent with Joseph Campbell's model of the Hero's Journey. When veterans return to society, the intention is to master two worlds — the military one we leave behind and the civilian world we seek to reenter. In doing so, we discover our deeper purpose in service to the whole of society. This is how we flourish in veteran life.

Once we recognize that flourishing is the intended outcome of our journey, we can accept that leaving the military is not about finding a job. It has nothing to do with LinkedIn profiles or a resume. It has everything to do with understanding who you are. This includes personal values, strengths, and purpose that fuel your internal drive. The military experience aligns with an individual's intrinsic motivation — it is not the source of that motivation. Once we understand what drives each of us on an individual level, we can find opportunities with the right engagement, meaning, fulfilling relationships, and worthwhile achievement for life beyond the military. We can find our version of flourishing. Only when we are at our best can we effectively serve society. That is when we answer the true nature of our calling.

When we joined the military, we were a lot like Danny — naive, innocent, and hopeful. We were just kids. When we return back to society we are not just older. We are not just wiser, either. We become different people entirely. We don't come back as Danny or the more adult version of Daniel you see in the modern *Cobra Kai* series on Netflix. We are not the karate kid, but the trusted mentor and guide for the next generation. We return as a version of Mr. Miyagi. Our responsibility is to empower others along their journey. Once you recognize this path, you can move forward. There is no going back. This psychological and spiritual imperative is essential for navigating your own successful return to society. With this foundation, let's apply Seligman's PERMA model to explore what it takes to flourish in life beyond the military.

CHAPTER 3

MEANING

"*I was there when the ambulance came," Jill said. Her voice was full of emotion, "You were gone."*

I didn't know what to say as Jill shared her experience from that morning. She found me less than a mile away from our house. I fell unconscious along the running trail just before the entrance to our small neighborhood.

The sequence of what happened was nothing short of a miracle. A construction worker on the roof in an adjacent development actually saw me fall. From the rooftop, he garnered the attention of a couple out walking along the trail. They ran to where I was on the ground. One person called 911 while the other began administering CPR. At the time, I had no pulse. A deputy from the St. John's County Sheriff's office arrived on the scene. Fortunately, she happened to have a defibrillator in her vehicle. She administered the first shock as St. John's

County Fire and Rescue arrived from a station just two miles away. EMS administered another shock, gave me a shot of Narcan, and pushed a few rounds of epinephrine. An EKG showed that my heart was now in supraventricular tachycardia (SVT). I had a pulse. I had come back from the dead. Any change in the sequence or timing of these events would have resulted in an entirely different ending.

As this was happening, Jill exited our neighborhood on her own morning run. She saw the commotion along the trail. Curiosity brought her to the circle of people standing over me. I can't hardly imagine what she must have felt when she realized that the person on the ground with his mouth open and eyes rolled to the back of his head was her husband.

EMS loaded me into the ambulance and Jill rode up front. I was unconscious on the way to the hospital. Both diaphoretic and vomiting, I was intubated along the way to keep my airway open. My ribs were bruised from the chest compressions and I had a collapsed lung. I don't remember any of this, but I'm certain Jill will never forget it.

As I disappeared into the Emergency Room of Baptist South in Jacksonville, Florida, Jill was left with the impossible responsibility of notifying family and friends. This included explaining to our children what had just happened to their dad.

I was the lucky one. Not just by how the circumstances unfolded that morning, but because I don't remember any of it. The ER staff placed me on a ventilator and swept me off to the Cath Lab. I woke up two days later to the handwritten note on the service tray. This was the nurse's way of attempting to reason with an unruly patient. In my brief moments of consciousness, I was defiant. Because of the trauma, I didn't know where I was or what was happening. At one point, I had disconnected the monitoring devices and ripped out my IV. I wanted to go home. I didn't consciously experience the nightmare and miracle of what transpired in the space of time between going out for a morning run and waking up in the hospital.

FINDING YOUR SENSE OF
PURPOSE AND MEANING

O ne thing we share as military leaders is the strong desire to make a difference. We want to contribute to something meaningful. This is what attracted us — at least in part — to this lifestyle of service. Departing the military means disconnecting from a purpose we identified with through most of our adult lives. Finding a sense of purpose and meaning on the other side of transition is a critical step — the center of gravity — for optimizing well-being in life beyond the military.

Let's face it. We were kids when we raised our right hand and swore the oath of service. I don't think anyone graduating from high school or college has a clear vision of what they really want to do with the rest of their lives. We were no exception. Most military leaders had no intention of staying beyond their initial service obligation (an observation validated through hundreds of conversations with senior leaders entering retirement). The plan was to do your time and find a real job, and yet here you are — decades later. Our reasons for joining don't explain why we stayed. Understanding what drove you to serve for so long in the military is the first clue to understanding what you might find meaningful in what happens next.

The hardest part of leaving the military is separating your personal identity from the identity provided by the uniform. This means identifying your values, recognizing your strengths, and finding your unique purpose. This is no small endeavor. The military gives you a set of values and a purpose while offering plenty of opportunities to showcase your strengths. You didn't need to understand your own personal mission because the military one suited you just fine. Understanding what you do, how you do it, and why you do it on an intrinsic level will help satisfy that hunger for meaning in life beyond the military.

Let's start with the values, and more specifically, your values. Values are innate, trait-like qualities shaped through education and experience. They provide the lens through which we see, interpret, and interact with the world around us. They operate on a subconscious level and shape everything we see and do — our attitudes, behaviors, and beliefs. We are drawn to people who align with our values and uncomfortable around those who don't. In the military, values are integral to our culture and development as leaders.

The good news is that our personal values align with those in the military. If they didn't, we would've left sooner rather than later. Because the military is so aggressive at integrating values in the character development of its leaders, it can be challenging to distinguish the difference between values that come with the uniform from those values that remain beyond the uniform.

Recognizing and understanding your values requires active reflection and introspection. In the book, *Beyond the Military: A Leader's Guide to Warrior Integration*, I provide an exercise to help guide this self-reflection for those who don't know where to start. It is important to understand how your values show up in different situations. This is the active part of the reflection. With practice, you can build your own cognitive routine to assess how a behavior, feeling, or action aligns with your values. You can be intentional about how to live a value centric life in the same way the military was intentional about how you integrated their values in the performance and execution of your duties. In doing so, you can make decisions and choices that are consistent with your character identity as a leader.

Like values, strengths are innate qualities that help define who you are as a leader. There are several ways to identify strengths largely because psychologists lack consensus on how to define them. One approach — character strengths — considers strengths as trait-like qualities that are integrated into your personality — almost like values. Where values represent a state of being, character strengths represent energizing qualities of your personality. Another approach — domain strengths — considers strengths as innate talents. These are the things that you do well because you find those activities energizing. As character traits or talents, there are a number of tools to recognize and apply your strengths.

The Values in Action (VIA) Institute on Character identified 24 distinctive qualities based on the virtues of courage, wisdom, transcendence, humanity, temperance, and justice. These strengths are "capacities for thinking, feeling, volition, and behaving. They are the psychological ingredients for displaying virtues and human goodness."[1] The research behind this approach for identifying strengths explored a wide variety of people from different cultures throughout history. The VIA Strengths Profile is an ipsative assessment that ranks the preponderance of these traits in an individual's personality. The top five strengths from this assessment describe your signature strengths — those qualities you bring forth naturally and allow you to perform at your best.

Another (and perhaps the most popular) resource for identifying strengths is the Clifton Strengths Finder. This

---

[1] Ryan M. Niemiec, *Mindfulness and Character Strengths: A Practical Guide to Flourishing* (Hogrefe Publishing, 2014), 26.

psychometric assessment measures talents — those naturally occurring patterns of thoughts, feelings, or behaviors.[2] The underlying premise for this approach is based on the fact that the human brain begins developing in the womb and continues until you reach 25 years of age. Strengths emerge as behaviors and activities we find naturally engaging. We want to do these activities, and because we do, we are drawn to those opportunities that allow us to apply and experience them. Based on the principle of neuroplasticity, the frequency, repetition, and intensity of those experiences stimulates neurological development. By the time we reach adulthood, these strengths have been hard-wired into the physiology of our brains.

Contrary to our upbringing in the military, focusing on strengths is far more effective than expending time and effort on our weaknesses. In the military, we tend to overlook the things we do well in search of what we do poorly. We gloss over the green bubbles of the stoplight chart and obsess about the red ones. The extensive research on this topic has been remarkably consistent: Those organizations that integrate a person's strengths into their job responsibilities show a substantial increase in performance and personal well-being. Organizations that integrate strengths create cultures where people want to come to work, are more committed to their jobs, and are far more productive. Strengths are the greatest asset to achieving meaningful and substantive outcomes. Recognizing and applying these qualities enable you to perform at your best and feel good while doing it.

Finally, we get to the question of your deeper purpose — your personal mission or the "why." This is the most elusive aspect of a person's identity. Many people will spend a

[2] Marcus Buckingham and Donald O. Clifton, *Now, Discover Your Strengths* (The Free Press, 2001), 29.

lifetime searching for purpose and meaning. Our spiritual nature yearns for a deeper connection to something beyond the mortal shell of our lives. It is the core theme for most of the world's religions (Christianity, Hinduism, Buddhism, Judaism, Islam), the foundation for prominent theories in psychology that includes Freud, Jung, Rank, Becker, and the guiding philosophy behind the previously referenced model of the Hero's Journey from Joseph Campbell. Because we join the military at such a young age, it is rather convenient to assume that military service is our purpose. It is not. The drive for psychological growth beyond self-actualization extends after your end of service date. The ultimate aspiration of human potential is individuation — enduring and meaningful contributions to the lives of others. This is the pinnacle of human endeavor that transcends our time in the military and the limitations of our mortality.

To become the "Hero" of your adventure, you must detach from the familiar standards of comfort and security to discover your own unique gift to bring into the world — the one that you and no other can offer humankind. In other words, you have to be willing to leap off the proverbial cliff if you ever hope to fly. The only path to flourish and achieve the ultimate boon of your life is through your purpose. Psychologically, it requires overcoming the social conventions that reinforce the perception of safety through the illusion of control. Spiritually, it requires transcendence — the passing away of one thing to allow the emergence and evolution of something better. Philosophically, it requires a meaningful integration of the past and transformation for apotheosis. Practically, it means letting go of the warrior identity to become something more as a veteran leader in society.

Unfortunately for each of us, the first step on the stairway to heaven is at the end of the highway to hell. This is a terrifying endeavor. So much so that many won't consider venturing out to discover or pursue their purpose. Many that do get stuck. They become paralyzed with fear and retreat back to the comfort defined by the standards of social convention. It's far easier to conform to the socially acceptable norms of a "good" life than it is to pursue a life well lived.

To put it another way, we settle. We choose the safest path and allow our true potential to wither with the passing of time. We ignore our spiritual yearning for a deeper sense of meaning in life. The material symbols of status and conveniences of comfort can ultimately suffocate our very soul. We have everything we need from psychoanalysis, depth psychology, religion, and philosophy to understand why. You were meant for something more than the material benefits, financial security, and accompanying social validation that comes from the accrual of wealth.

You got a taste of that in the military. You weren't doing it for the money. Once you've been exposed to life experiences of meaning and purpose, everything else pales in comparison. This is especially true of combat veterans who have touched the limits of humanity. You've seen behind the curtain of life. When you bear witness to the sacrifice that comes from service, more secular endeavors measured by a paycheck or stock options don't have the same appeal.

On the other side of the military adventure is the potential for personal transformation. Combat will change your life's narrative — forever. This is not necessarily a bad thing. Exposure to trauma and the limits of the human condition can offer increased strength and resilience, stronger and more meaningful relationships, increased spirituality with a renewed appreciation for life, and — as a result of an evolved narrative — new opportunities. If you have enough faith to take that leap, the military adventure is a catalyst for hope and inspiration in a future role that improves society as a whole.

What you've experienced in the military is part of a deeper sacrifice that comes with the obligation of service. Everything you have seen, everything you have done, and every emotion you have felt has been entrusted to you. You have a responsibility to repurpose the totality of that experience to guide, inspire, and lead society. This is the burden on the other side of military service — one that nobody tells you about when you first volunteered, but one you will carry with you for the rest of your life.

The adventure into the unknown world will shatter any innocence by challenging the core foundation of your beliefs. Growth requires a dialectical approach that appreciates the inherent paradox between beliefs and reality and integrates both into a new worldview — one that reconciles belief with lived experience into knowledge and wisdom for a renewed vision of service in society.

Finding purpose from all you have experienced in the military is not easy, but failure to do so can be catastrophic. Society has classified this phenomenon by different names throughout history — melancholia, combat stress, battle fatigue, combat neurosis, moral injury, and — of course — PTSD. Although the names have changed over time, the symptoms have remained the same: emotional disorders characterized by a depressive state with varying degrees of anxiety, fear, guilt, shame, and regret. Does any of this sound familiar? This is the path to despair. It explains why so many veterans struggle in civilian life. This is what happens when you cannot reconcile what you believe with what you have experienced. We treat veteran suicide as an emergent crisis from the most recent conflict, but these demons have always haunted the space between service in the military and life on the other side. We spend too much time talking about the problem instead of the opportunity — the potential for post-traumatic growth and positive transformation. Understanding the possibilities begins by understanding your true purpose.

Your military experience provides important clues for discovering that purpose. You had at least some alignment between your personal mission and the military mission. If you didn't, you wouldn't have stayed as long as you did. With the benefit of hindsight, challenge yourself to recreate the mission statement for what you achieved throughout the duration of your career — from your first day wearing a uniform through retirement, independent of the role or duty position. I am not talking about a military mission from one of your units. I am talking about YOUR mission. Think about it from the perspective of the 5 W's — *who, what, where, when,* and *why.* We'll also add in *how.* The *who* is you, *where* is wherever the military sent you, and *when* is your period of service. These are known. The three remaining elements — *what* you do, *how* you do it, and *why* you do it — require deeper reflection and define your unique purpose.

What you do has an internal locus of causality — meaning that you are intrinsically motivated to do this activity regardless of title or role. It describes what you do when you show up to any organization. Here is a hint — it is not leading or serving. Leading and serving are outcomes based on what you do. Go deeper. Examples of what you do may include one or more of the following: inspire, explore, grow, expand, connect, empower, discover, motivate, build, create, honor, protect, elevate, optimize, or fulfill. These are anabolic action words. They apply to people, ideas, potential, teams, opportunities, etc. When we combine the action and the object of that action, we define *what* you do. To inspire others, to discover opportunities, to build potential, to connect people and ideas, or to optimize outcomes are just a few examples of how to define *what* you do.

Your values and strengths drive *how* you do anything. The interplay of strengths and values creates the synergy for powerful action. Your challenge is to piece together the puzzle of how you leverage these qualities to contribute to the world around you. Let's look at an example using strengths from the Clifton Strengths Finder: If *relator* is one of your talents, then building meaningful relationships is probably something you do well. If *ideation* and *winning others over* are also strengths of yours, then the combination of these qualities might suggest that you generate momentum (*winning others over*) for creative ideas (*ideation*) through meaningful relationships (*relator*). How you do something should be both personally invigorating and come naturally at the same time.

Finally, we get to the *why* — or the impact you want to achieve. Understanding the reasons you stayed in the military is the key to discovering your deeper purpose. Reflect on the high points of your career and consider the impact that you achieved in terms of the people, the mission, and the organization. As you do, you may begin to uncover some recurring themes — to empower others, elevate potential, bridge gaps, transform systems, maximize effectiveness, achieve elite performance outcomes, build an enduring legacy of future leaders, etc. Consider how you notice the impact you've had on an organization as you're leaving. As you begin to see patterns, you may start to understand what makes an achievement meaningful to you.

Purpose is the combination of these elements: What you do: *To inspire leaders.* How you do it: *by integrating unique capabilities and imagination.* Why you do it: *to bridge the gap between confidence and potential.* When you put the who, what, and the how together, you have a mission statement:

To inspire leaders by integrating unique capabilities and imagination for bridging the gap between confidence and potential.

I describe this as an "initial" purpose because we've only looked at your time in the military. This is just a sample of your life. Think of this statement as a hypothesis — your best guess to define what drives you. In order to test this hypothesis, reflect on those moments when you most enjoyed the work you were doing and when you were at your best. Compare what you did, how you did it, and the impact you had against your purpose statement. Use your experience to refine this statement so it more accurately describes what you've done and accomplished throughout your career.

Once you become aware of your mission, you can be more consciously competent about how you might apply it moving forward. Once you see the path based on where you've been, you can look forward to where it might go. Your refined purpose statement becomes the standard against which you compare future opportunities.

On a practical level, you can do this through networking. Ask open ended questions that explore how well the organization or role aligns with your personal mission statement. Invite people to talk about their experiences in their own words. Stay away from corporate messaging and talking points. Assess the quality of how their experience aligns with your unique mission. Think of this as a form of targeting. You are searching for actionable intelligence to drive your decision for future opportunities.

This cognitive exercise has the potential for lifelong benefits. The process of filtering opportunities against your individual purpose is a routine that — over time — can become a habit. When it does, you will subconsciously evaluate opportunities and decisions outside the military in the same way you did the mission and commander's intent throughout your career. You become intentional about how the choices you make align with what you find meaningful. You can start living on purpose and uncover opportunities to flourish in veteran life.

CHAPTER 4

POSITIVE EMOTION

I *met the cardiologist the next day. He was a middle-aged gentleman who spoke with a thick Indian accent. He was very kind and mild mannered. He offered some pleasantries as he slid the diaphragm of his stethoscope to different points across my chest and abdomen. Once he completed this cursory examination, he affirmed and reiterated what the nurse told me from the day before. I had a heart attack, and I was lucky to be alive.*

When I asked him about how he cleared the blockage, he pulled out a tablet and showed me the video replay of the catheterization. I got to witness both before and after the stent was inserted into my left anterior descending artery. I saw the extent of the blockage and the corresponding reopening of the artery.

As the video played, he drew my attention to the network of blood vessels around my heart. It was at this point that he introduced me to the phenomena of angiogenesis. He explained that this was how the body adapts to blockages by building its own bypasses around coronary obstructions. These new vessels provided the blood flow to keep my heart beating when it went into cardiac arrest. Because heart tissue dies rapidly when deprived of oxygen, he said that this was the only reason why I was still alive. This explains the low survival rate (around 12 percent) for this type of cardiac event and validates the "widow maker" nickname.

We discussed my medical history. As far back as I could remember, there was no record of cardiovascular or related heart disease from either side of my family. Quite to the contrary, I had a strong legacy of exceptional cardiovascular health. Admittedly, I had times when my cholesterol was high, but my most recent blood work from just a few days earlier was excellent. I didn't have any physical symptoms. I wasn't tired. I had no chest pain or shortness of breath. I was running as much as 20 miles a week and working out extensively. There were no obvious precursors to this near fatal event.

The doctor told me that not all heart conditions have a physical origin. He noted that I had been diagnosed with an anxiety disorder, one of the unwanted stowaways that I brought home from my final deployment. He asked me about the Xanax that appeared in my lab work since I had no active prescription for this medication. I told him that the pills belonged to my wife, and I took them to help me sleep at night. I was constantly haunted by nightmares. I would routinely sweat through the sheets with frequent outbursts and muffled screams. I would awaken often in the darkness in the throes of sheer panic. Xanax was my choice of self-medication that helped me get through the night.

Anxiety was a condition that impacted so many aspects of my life. I could not operate an automobile at night in unfamiliar places. I had difficulty driving over large bridges, and I would not — under any circumstances — get behind the driver's wheel while traveling through the mountains. The last time that I did, I experienced a severe panic attack and could barely recover the car safely. Aidan, my five year old son at the time, slept peacefully in the back seat. I could have killed us both. I didn't trust myself to drive in those situations anymore.

When I was finished explaining myself, the doctor told me that mental and emotional distress were as significant a factor to poor cardiovascular health as was a steady diet of cheesesteaks and french fries. This was particularly true for veterans. Studies showed that combat veterans were six times more likely to suffer cardiovascular and heart disease than their nonveteran counterparts. I had no idea that this was the case, but I started to understand the cause for my current health condition: Mental and emotional distress had a deadly, physical manifestation in the blood vessels around my heart.

THE HAPPY VETERAN

*W*hat does it mean to be truly happy in life after military service? How do we get rid of the stubborn baggage that comes back with us when we return from combat? Happiness is not one of the benefits included in your retirement package. In fact, too many veterans experience the exact opposite. For proof you only need to look at the higher rates of addiction, mental health issues, and suicide when compared to our nonveteran counterparts. Too many of our brothers and sisters are not only unhappy, but they are suffering in plain sight. For as long as we have been sending men and women into combat, the veteran community has been battling demons in a silent state of despair.

Too many veterans assume that they won't find the same level of fulfillment and satisfaction that they once enjoyed in the military. Consequently, they just settle for a job. They stagnate in professional malaise devoid of inspiration. Add in the mental and emotional challenges from combat service, and you have the perfect storm to explain the ongoing well-being challenges in the veteran community. Perhaps the reason why so many veterans are languishing is because they simply don't know how to find joy in ordinary life.

Joy is but one of several positive emotions connected to our subjective well-being — modern psychology's term for "happiness." In addition to joy, psychologists have recognized gratitude, serenity, interest, hope, pride, amusement, inspiration, awe, and love as the most common positive emotions. We experience these emotions in varying degrees at different points throughout our military careers. We are exposed to memorable events that evoke inspiration and a sense of awe. We share a deep feeling of pride for our unit and the higher purpose of our mission. We love our sisters and brothers in arms like family. We find interesting the changing and challenging nature of the work. We experience so many positive emotions on a regular basis through the military journey. The fact that we don't notice moments of joy isn't a big deal — until we leave.

We become so focused and preoccupied with our obligations to the unit that we simply don't notice singular moments that bring us joy. This isn't entirely our fault. The nature of successful leadership in the post 9/11 world hinders our ability and cognitive capacity to experience many positive emotions — most notably serenity, gratitude, and joy. Veterans are not wired to experience positive emotions in the otherwise fleeting moments of our daily consciousness, and therefore, the idea of joy becomes an elusive construct in life beyond the military.

Generally speaking, happiness doesn't come from signature life events or material treasures. Studies have shown that the happiness we draw from holidays, graduations, or the birth of a child tends to decay rapidly. After an initial burst of excitement, we return to a steady state of emotional homeostasis which may or may not include joy. Happiness is not a trophy won after you've worked your whole life, funded your children's education, and paid off your mortgage. The rise in financial standing across our country has been met with a commensurate decrease in emotional and mental wellness over the past 50 years. The burden of achieving and maintaining a certain economic and social status actually makes people less happy.

Happiness is not something that can be seized and controlled like key terrain as part of a military operation. What we have learned through the study of positive psychology is that happiness — a true sense of joy — comes from ordinary moments in our everyday lives. Joy comes from what is around us. It is watching your children grow, feeling your partner's hand in yours, and sharing expressions of love with family and friends. Finding happiness requires a certain state of mind, and it doesn't come with a price tag. In order to find happiness, you have to set an intention to notice it — a task that is much easier said than done for military leaders.

Military leaders are not calibrated to appreciate or even recognize the positive. In fact, we are trained and conditioned to do the exact opposite. Our job is to identify and solve problems before they compromise the mission and endanger our people. We excel in the application of risk management. We are practitioners of a phenomenon known as defensive pessimism — the ability to identify potential vulnerabilities or weaknesses and take proactive and preventative measures to ensure unimpeded progress toward desired outcomes. We find problems before they become problems. This is what we do. It is a fundamental requirement of the job. Unfortunately, defensive pessimism becomes a habit that bleeds into every aspect of life whether it involves planning a military operation or a weekend vacation with your family.

When you go looking for problems, you tend to find them. The ability to prevent failure does not guarantee success. Stated another way, the absence of despair does not guarantee happiness. Consider a scenario where you are tasked to count the number of red cars that you see on your morning commute into work. When you arrive at the office, you expect your boss to ask you how many red cars you saw, but instead, they ask you how many green cars you noticed along the commute. You are certain you passed green cars, but you have no idea how many. You weren't paying attention to the green cars. You were too busy counting the red ones. Psychologists call this inattentional blindness. It isn't that moments of joy aren't there. Just like the green cars from your morning commute, you just don't notice them.

Another handicap comes from the perpetual state of hyperawareness and overstimulation that is reinforced through the military experience. Emotions like serenity, gratitude, and joy demand conscious attention in the here and now of the moment. Unfortunately, presence is not something we do well. Our ability to manage multiple, competing, and often overlapping tasks in dynamic and ambiguous environments is an essential quality of successful military leadership. Being in the moment risks the opportunity to get ahead of a future problem — even one that currently doesn't exist.

Given the nature of the challenges we face, we value

the ability to sift through volumes of information, conduct rapid analysis, and make sound decisions in dynamic, constrained, and even dangerous environments. As an army aviator, I learned this skill during flight school. In the cockpit, this was known as the cross-check. With hands on the controls and feet on the pedals, new pilots learn how to rapidly glance at more than a dozen instruments and systems on the front display panel and return their focus outside the aircraft. They process what they saw in that moment while scanning the horizon for obstacles or navigation cues. Safely staying ahead of the aircraft requires that we master the ability to process more than what we see and notice in the moment.

Once pilots master this under daytime conditions, they are trained to do it at night. Pilots apply a series of visual cues to safely maneuver a helicopter at high speeds as near as possible to the surface of the earth. Then, we add five radios squawking in your ears simultaneously. Then, we put you in charge of not one, but an entire flight of aircraft as a mission commander. Then, you get deployed and have to do this in some of the harshest flight environments on the planet. Once you've shown you can do this at the highest level, someone starts shooting at you. This training began at the onset of my military journey and was reinforced throughout the duration of my career. This was my experience, but I believe every branch and operating specialty has their own version of training this form of high octane multitasking.

This valuable skill becomes a curse. As a result of this behavioral conditioning, we never truly break away from the myriad of challenges we face on a routine basis. We are afraid that we might miss something. You can always spot a military leader at a little league baseball game by their grooming standards and also because they are constantly checking their phones. I'll bet that the first thing you reach for in the morning on a day off is your work phone. You want to see if anything bad happened the night before. Read that sentence again. The first thing we do with the promise of a new day is go looking for something negative from the past. Honestly, have you ever expected to see good news in the unread messages from the night before? Let's face it, being present and focusing our attention on the here and now are not things we tend to do well.

This hyperactive state of mental cognition is analogous to the frequency hop mode of secure radio communications. We are constantly shifting our focus from one thing to another every few seconds. Over the duration of a career, this activity becomes ingrained in our subconscious. Our brains construct the neural pathways to perform these actions more efficiently. With these habits hardwired into our physiology, we become extremely sensitive to incoming stimuli with the instinctive ability to bounce — or frequency hop — rapidly from one task to another. This may help explain why so many veterans struggle with anxiety. Add in a few deployments and this state of anxiety becomes a permanent state of being. Even though we say that we want to slow down when we transition from the military, our brains are simply not calibrated to do so.

In the military, this works. It allows us to expand our capacity and capability to meet the responsibility for everything our command does or fails to do. Our culture is one where the team depends on *our* self-actualization. We have to be at our best. We experience a sense of satisfaction based on the success of the team. Shared accomplishments are professionally motivating and personally rewarding. We push the boundaries of our potential because it reinforces our measure of esteem and belonging to the team. We feel like worthy contributors to something greater than ourselves. Despite the hazardous nature of the work, our ability to do more and do better infuses a sense of hope — the positive emotion that sustains and drives us through the most difficult challenges. The synergy of emotional benefits make a strong case to stay in the military and make it a career.

The rush of chemicals from the release of hormones and neurotransmitters coursing through our systems as a result of our culture can be intoxicating. We call it camaraderie. When we depart this culture, the tide from this once overflowing sea of positive emotion begins to recede, and we feel alone. In place of those positive emotions is a certain emptiness that longs for connection, sense of meaning, and engagement. Finding happiness on the other side of military service isn't about preventing the tide of positive emotion from receding, but finding new sources of nourishment coming in.

The practice of mindfulness is one way to recondition yourself to focus on the present. Mindfulness has been proven to slow, expand, and even heal the mind. It can help warriors find a measure of peace, serenity, gratitude, and joy when they come home. By coaching veterans on the ability to be more mindful, we help them be more present. They can switch the busy mind from frequency hop to single channel mode and slow down.

Some of the interventions that improve mindfulness include journaling, breathing exercises, mindful walking or running, body scans, meditation, cognitive reframing, and practicing acceptance and appreciation. These are not touchy-feely suggestions but rather evidence-based approaches that have been proven to increase well-being and performance. Given the time you've spent reinforcing the frequency hop mode of mindless intentions, integrating these practices into your routine won't happen overnight.

For example, journaling about gratitude involves recording positive moments throughout the day on a routine basis. Doing so shifts your attention from the negative and "what could go wrong" to appreciate "what is right and well in your world." In the beginning, it may be difficult to notice these positive moments. Think of it like trying to learn how to write with your non-dominant hand. It takes time. After a few months of disciplined practice, you may notice that you have cataloged dozens if not hundreds of positive thoughts, emotions, and behaviors that occur on a routine basis throughout the day. You can still be an expert in finding the red cars, and now you've developed the ability to notice the green ones as well.

Meditation can be more rewarding but also more challenging as a new practice. It might be hard to sit still and focus your attention on one thing for any period of time. If this is the case, start with shorter periods of time. If you can't concentrate on your breathing for five minutes, start with one minute. It only gets easier with practice. Over time, you'll notice that the act of "centering" yourself requires less effort. A sense of serenity begins to occupy the space once dominated by hyperarousal. You recalibrate the mind to hold space and gain access to the emotions — joy, serenity, and gratitude — that reside in the moment.

It is harder to slow the mind later in life than it was to speed it up early in your career. This has to do with the neurology of adult development. Because the brain is still developing until we reach 25 years of age, many habits associated with hyperarousal and a negative mindset are hard-wired into our physiology. Consequently, forming or changing habits becomes increasingly more difficult as we breach the threshold of middle age. According to Dr. Joe Dispenza, an adult's personality is 95 percent formed by the time we reach the age of 35. That means that if you stayed in the military beyond the age of 30, most of your adult persona and the very physiology of your brain was shaped through the military culture. Your habits were forged in an environment that is strikingly different from the norms of civilian society. Returning to the ordinary world requires the remaining 5 percent of conscious intention to create new habits. Recent research suggests that the average time it takes to form a new habit can vary between 18 and 254 days with older adults tending to lean on the long side of that scale. As old dogs, we are perfectly capable of learning new tricks, but it takes us longer to do so.

Mindfulness requires time, patience, and dedication in the same way that you needed training and lived experiences to develop the risk management and multitasking skills to succeed as a military leader. That said, this is the path to expanding how you experience positive emotions in life beyond the military. It will be challenging — but not impossible — to find the same level of interest, awe, pride, amusement, and inspiration that we experienced in the military adventure. Finding a role that aligns with your values, strengths, and purpose is a good start. Investing the time and energy to stack mindfulness habits in life as a veteran will answer the questions about how and where to find happiness. In doing so, you may find something else that tends to evade too many struggling veterans . . . hope on the other side of military service.

CHAPTER 5

ENGAGEMENT & RELATIONSHIPS

*T*he next time I saw the cardiologist was on the day I was discharged from the hospital. I had to enroll in a program for physical therapy and cardiac rehabilitation. He was recommending that I sign up for the Ornish Lifestyle Medicine program. This is the only program of rehabilitation proven to reverse cardiovascular disease. The Ornish program integrates mental, emotional, and nutritional wellness with physical therapy. This was a substantial commitment that included 12, four-hour sessions every Tuesday and Thursday for nine weeks. It combined monitored physical activity with facilitated group sessions for emotional wellness, mindfulness, and nutrition.

I was skeptical. I mean, did I really need to invest that much time into my rehabilitation? I didn't have any other arterial blockages, and the stent solved the one problem I did have. It seemed a bit much to me. I preferred an easier — or less involved — path.

I shared these thoughts with my doctor. As I did, his demeanor changed. "You have been given a gift that not many people in your situation get," he said. "What you have been through in your life was significant enough to have killed you. You got lucky — this time. You need to decide what you want from life on the other side."

"The other side?" I was confused. So I asked, "Meaning the other side of the heart attack or my life as a veteran?"

He shrugged his shoulders, paused for a moment and said, "Perhaps both." He turned as if he was going to walk out of the room and looked back at me to say "I wonder if the reason why you avoid the mental and emotional side of your health is the very reason why you are *here now."*

I didn't have a response. I sat in silence as I waited for my family to pick me up and take me home.

DOING GOOD WORK WITH GOOD PEOPLE

*A*t the risk of making a rash generalization, most military leaders — myself included — want to solve problems and help people. That's what we enjoyed in the military, and that is what we want to continue doing after we leave. We are drawn to wicked hard problems. We don't want to work for a company that cares only about profit. We want to do good work. We also want to find the "right" culture — you know, like what we had in the military. We want to work with good people. How do you find the right opportunity when your criteria is doing good work with good people?

In the military, the specifics of the job didn't really matter. Where we went and what we did were driven largely by the needs of the service. After we report to a new duty station, we are placed in roles where we typically have little or no experience or expertise. We are expected to figure it out. We apply a baseline set of skills and talents to adapt and learn on the job. Over time, we become competent in that role. Our confidence grows. Once we've mastered that role, we are reassigned to another unfamiliar role. We start over. We take what we've learned from the previous job and apply it to the next one. We repeat this cycle in one or two year increments throughout our careers.

Unlike our civilian counterparts, the military doesn't rely on functional competence for career progression. Their objective is to develop your identity as a leader. The military bets on potential. New experiences with expanding responsibilities are designed to develop a leader's personal and professional identity. New challenges from unfamiliar roles push us to the outer limits of our comfort zone. This develops confidence to show up and lead regardless of the situation.

Consequently, we've honed an ability to rapidly learn and adapt to new roles in different situations. Mastering your job in a way that contributes to the mission is — in and of itself — personally rewarding. You can be satisfied with your work contribution even if you are generally unsatisfied with the nature of the work. Over the course of a career, you feel good about the prospect of walking into any job and finding a way to solve problems and help people provided you were working in the right culture to do so.

When you leave the military, the expectations change. Job function matters more. You should know what industry you want to join. You are supposed to know what company you want to work for. You should already know what position you want and be qualified to meet the requirements for that particular role. When you think about it, this is the exact opposite approach from how you've navigated your career in the military. So, how do you take the way that you've approached jobs for years or even decades and overlay that with the process of finding the right job in the civilian world? The answer is: Don't focus on the job, focus on you. More specifically, focus on the kinds of things you really want to do and the kind of people you want to be with.

Define what you want to do based on those activities

that you find engaging, fulfilling, and meaningful. Consider situations throughout your career when you experienced flow. Flow is a construct in positive psychology that describes a state of consciousness that is all consuming. These are intrinsically motivating activities that you would choose to do regardless of how much you might get paid to do them. We reach a state of flow when the nature of the challenge we face is at the upper limit of our perceived skills. They include those stretch opportunities outside our comfort zone. Flow is the point where performance, engagement, and personal satisfaction come together. When in "the flow," you tend to be at your very best and feel good about it at the same time.

Go beyond the title or position and get into the details about the specific activities — the things you actually spent your time doing. Think about those work circumstances when you would volunteer to show up early or stay late. Consider the problem sets and solution approaches that you found invigorating. Perhaps you valued those situations when you had to leverage creativity, logic, numerical analysis, imagination, open collaboration, incremental progress, huge payoffs, or a combination of these characteristics. Understand how you applied your strengths to persevere and achieve in those situations when you were outside your comfort zone. Think about the kinds of problems that the boss keeps sending your way regardless of whether or not you ask for them. Identify the times when you were most energized at work and recognize the factors that contributed to your excitement. Consider what made a contribution meaningful in terms of how it impacted the people, the organization, or the mission.

Start at the beginning of your career and walk through your most recent job. See if you can identify three examples of positive qualities from each role or duty assignment. List all of the things you were doing that put you in that state of flow. Once you have walked through the entirety of your military career, you have a detailed description of all the things that you really want to do. In essence, you have just created the ideal job description independent of any particular role or duty position.

Now that you know what you are looking for, let's go out and find it. You probably won't find a job description that reads point by point down the list you just created, but you have a template of what you are looking for. You've developed a targeting matrix to discover the ideal opportunity based on what you find most engaging. You can discover the specific role or organization that best aligns with your targeting plan through the networking process. Ask probing and open-ended questions. Be thought provoking in conversations and stay away from questions that have a "yes" or "no" answer. As you learn about opportunities and organizations through this process, continue to refine your list in the same way you would update your collection plan or targeting matrix in the military.

If you want more work-life balance, be sure to add everything that you want to happen on a routine basis outside the workplace. Consider what you want to do before you start working and what you would like to do at the end of the day. Include those activities that would fill your tank across the physical, mental, emotional, and spiritual domains. Be intentional about what happens on your off time. If you don't, you risk falling back into what you know — a workaholic lifestyle that resembles what you experienced through the military.

Now, let's go back to those positive emotions that you want to experience throughout the day. Take a look at the complete list of daily activities and highlight where and when you would experience any of those positive emotions. If you can model this for an average workday, you've mapped out your ideal lifestyle.

A full-time employee in the United States will work approximately 260 days a year. The other 105 days are weekends, holidays, and other fun stuff. If you can identify what you want to experience both professionally and personally on an average Tuesday, you will probably be satisfied with your life. Notice also that we didn't talk about specific times of the day. We were not constrained by the clock. We didn't squeeze the white space out of the schedule in the same way we do when synchronizing calendars in the military. We simply explored how to optimize your personal and professional life. From this perspective, you can see how a job supports the desired lifestyle instead of how it works in the military where the job comes first, your family gets the leftovers, and you are left with the crumbs that fall to the floor. Through this application of solution focused coaching, you can outline what flourishing looks like to you.

Now that you have an idea of what you want to do, let's figure out who you want to do it with. An important lesson we learn in the military is that what we are doing is not as important as who we are doing it with. The quality of the people improves the quality of the experience — especially during times of hardship. Based on your career, consider how you would define the qualities of the ideal colleague — people you would be interacting with on a regular basis. How would you describe them in terms of intellect, values, communication style, personality, interests, or any other attributes that come to mind? If you are going to spend about a third of your life on the job, you might want to be somewhat discerning about the people you are spending that time with. They should include people you enjoy being around that also bring out the best in you.

Given your experience, identify those organizational traits that you believe are essential for a high performance culture. The right fit is a function of shared values, common purpose, and a supportive environment that enables and encourages you to thrive. If diversity is a quality you value, think about how that quality shows up in terms of collaboration and problem solving. If you value continuous learning, explore the ways that an organization encourages learning and development across the workforce. Assess how the organization responds to a setback — do they punish failure or learn from it? If creativity and innovation are important to you, ask about new ideas, approaches, and products under development. If you value empowerment, find out how people are rewarded or punished for taking the initiative. If you believe that compassion and empathy are important leadership qualities, then you may want to know some of the ways that leaders from the organization demonstrate compassion to the workforce. If you want to have fun on the job, then you might want to pay attention to the general mood of employees as you walk around. Culture is something that you experience, so you won't find these answers on the internet. You have to speak directly with the people in the organization to understand what the culture is really like.

Now that you've been able to assess the people and culture of the organization, consider how that organization contributes to the community or society as a whole. If you want to be part of something bigger than the bottom line, understand how the organization is working to make the world a better place. Take a look at the population they want to serve through their products and services. Find out what people find inspiring about their work and listen to real testimonials from the people they've served. See what they have to say about how the organization has impacted them. Find an organization that shares your inspiration to serve the population or market segment that you find meaningful in the ways that you want to make a difference.

Flourishing is something particular to the individual, so if that is your objective, start with you. You have an entire career of experiences to inform what you find most engaging with the relationships you most desire in a professional setting. Use what you've learned about yourself throughout your military career to define your standard of doing good work with good people.

CHAPTER 6

ACHIEVEMENT

I *was excited to see my family. Alone in a hospital room is a foreboding existence. Hospital protocol required that I depart in a wheelchair. I preferred to walk out on my own. I was nervous. I wanted to assure my family that I was okay, and I also needed some assurance for myself.*

I don't know what I was expecting from this particular homecoming. I had done a number of emotional reunions throughout my career — most notably from multiple combat deployments to Afghanistan. Each one was special because a year is a long time to be away from a family with growing children.

I had little doubt that I would come home after each trip to Afghanistan. I think all military leaders share some misguided beliefs about our mortality or immortality — as appropriate. It is part of the coping mechanism that allows us to keep doing the things we are asked to do in the very dangerous places we are asked to do them.

This time was different. Death wasn't an unrealistic possibility. It happened. I actually died. "Sudden cardiac death" was a label forever engraved in the records of my medical history. According to the percentages, I shouldn't be here. This wasn't emotional longing from an extended separation. It was a miracle.

I was overwhelmed when I saw Jill and the boys. I couldn't wait to get my arms around them. If it was uncool for teenage boys to express emotion for their parents in public, I didn't care. I remember grabbing a hold of Jill, and I can't remember letting go. More than any other deployment I had experienced, I couldn't wait to get home.

That was when I made my decision to attend the most intensive program of cardiac rehabilitation. The doctor's argument was compelling, but he wasn't nearly as convincing as my family. I don't know if I will ever understand what I put them through, but I didn't want to do that again.

I felt like George Bailey from It's A Wonderful Life. *I got a glimpse behind the curtain of what life might be like if I wasn't around. Throughout my military career, I was so focused on the mission and the next deployment that I never really considered what would have happened if I didn't come home. This impacted me in ways that are difficult to describe. More than ever, I knew that I had a responsibility to be present for my family. I had to do my part. They needed me. Over the next month, I would start the rehabilitation process for life after death.*

THE ODYSSEY HOME:
A NEW STATE OF BEING

*L*eaving the military is somewhat anticlimactic. Any pageantry ends when you drive out the main gate for the last time. Your status changes from member to veteran. There are no more morning formations. There are no more uniforms. You can actually let your hair grow out. Perhaps the biggest challenge you might face will be how to match your shirt with your slacks before you leave the house for work in the morning. For all the hustle and bustle leading up to your separation, leaving the military is somewhat underwhelming.

The most important aspects of transition are the parts you can't see. Military transition is an evolution into a new state of being. It is extremely difficult but also something you are completely capable of doing. It requires embracing who you are, understanding what you do, and knowing the deeper reason why you are here. In the best case scenario, it means flourishing — living your best life on both a personal and professional level to contribute to society in a meaningful way. In this context, achievement is not an objective. It is the culmination of your adventure into a new state of being.

As Joseph Campbell outlined in the Hero's Journey, returning to the ordinary world comes with its own challenges. First, there is a refusal to return. We don't want to go back. We want to stay with our band of brothers and sisters. We value our shared identity and sense of belonging. Second, we have to navigate the divide between the military world we are departing and the civilian one we are joining. For many of us, this can be the scariest part of the journey. Third, your leaders don't understand this process because they have no frame of reference. This is typically the first thing you experience before your boss does. Help comes from those guides and mentors from the civilian world. Most importantly, we can't go back to the past and be what we once were. Forward movement requires that we become something more.

This transformation is a highly intimate process. It doesn't happen with prepared slides delivered in a classroom setting over five days. It took Ulysses more than a decade to return home after the Trojan War, and each of us embarks upon our own odyssey back to ordinary society when we begin the transition process.

This particular part of your adventure can be more treacherous than anything you faced on the battlefield. It transcends the mere physical. The shadow of your experience torments you along the way. These experiences can be integrated in a healthy way or metastasize into something more pernicious. Veterans who struggle to reconcile all aspects of who they are — the good, the bad, and the ugly — tend to lose their way. They may leave the military, but they never make it home.

At the end of this odyssey, the prospect of flourishing awaits. It is a much more valuable prize than just finding a job. It is a higher state of psychological well-being. Nobody can tell you how to get there. You have to discover it for yourself. This is the path to individuation, sharing the wisdom to lead and serve society after military service. This is your hero's journey.

This chapter explores achievement in the context of *meaningful* employment. What I can offer are observations and lessons learned based on more than 3500 one-on-one conversations with over 650 men and women like you who once stood at the threshold between military service and life on the other side. These are guideposts for your consideration as you navigate your journey home:

- People Matter More than Paper
- The Networking Paradox
- Networking Lines of Effort
- False Flags
- Certification Constraints
- Personal Branding
- Telling Stories that Matter
- Understanding the True Meaning of Loyalty

Let's explore each of these in more detail to best prepare you for the journey back to the ordinary world.

People Matter More than Paper

The resume is a sounding gun that begins the race for finding a new job. Consequently, it becomes a convenient excuse to delay putting yourself out there. One thing I've learned in the transition space is that the value of your resume is inversely proportional to your rank and time in service. The higher your rank and years served, the less significant your resume is to finding a meaningful job opportunity. For military leaders searching for their next career, relationships are far more important than resumes.

Personal referrals through networking are the most effective way that experienced leaders find the most attractive career opportunities. Positions of leadership and significance in any organization depend as much (and in many cases more) on fit and reputation as they do your work experience and job qualifications. Senior leaders and executive hiring managers want to know what they're getting before entrusting an outsider with any meaningful amount of authority and responsibility. Conversations through networking are far more valuable to the job search than word-smithing your experience and education into one to two pages or listing abbreviations after your name on your LinkedIn profile.

One of the misguided assumptions leaders make in the transition process is that their network is limited to the people with whom they served. They believe that they don't know anyone outside their specific branch or specialty. This limiting belief reveals a fundamental misunderstanding of the networking process. The people *you* already know are just the starting point.

Networking is about expanding your circle of allies — leveraging the people you know to connect with the people they know. It is normal to feel vulnerable and somewhat uncomfortable in the beginning, this is why it is best to start with the people you already know. Activating your network means alerting your inner circle of colleagues, mentors, former supervisors, and previous subordinates about your intentions to leave the service. You should include friends and extended family as well. They may not work in an organization or industry of particular interest to you, but they may know someone who does. You have no idea who they know in their network, and they could prove to be an invaluable resource expanding the bench of allies for your next job. This is how you build a network to find the right opportunity.

You can begin this process at any time. Everyone has to leave the military at some point, and building relationships can provide access to people and opportunities that you don't even know exist. Update your contact list before you begin filling out a resume. Start with the beginning of your career up to your present duty assignment. Don't let the idea of building a resume keep you from the most effective strategy for finding meaningful opportunities in life beyond the military. For experienced military leaders looking for the next career opportunity, people matter more than paper.

The Networking Paradox

The idea of networking can be uncomfortable and intimidating. Asking someone else for assistance is not your thing. We spend a career being the person other people came to for help. We don't like being the one asking for assistance. We certainly don't want to burden those leaders and mentors we respect. On a personal level, we don't want them to think we can't handle this on our own.

What is remarkable about this scenario is how our feelings change when the roles are reversed. If anyone we had worked with throughout our career reached out to us for assistance, we'd be thrilled. We'd consider it an honor that they chose us and valued our input during this very vulnerable time in their lives. We see it as a form of validation for our impact as leaders. For many of us, it would be the highlight of our day!

Therein lies the paradox. If we do the asking, it is an inconvenience or a show of weakness, but if someone else is asking the same from us, we consider it a privilege. If you wouldn't see this as a burden or inconvenience, then trust that others won't either. In most cases, they want to reconnect as much as you do. Just like you, they would be honored that you thought of them. So, write the email, make the call, or send the text, and when you land that job, remember to be there for those leaders and mentees who will inevitably cross over into the civilian world behind you.

Networking Lines of Effort

As mentioned earlier, networking is an activity that you can do at any time. It is not reserved for the last year of service before separation. You don't have to target a particular industry. You don't need to focus on a specific role. Networking can occur if you know exactly what you want to do or when you have no idea what you're looking for. There are different levels of networking along three lines of effort that include discovery, informational, and interview networking.

Discovery networking is the best approach when you have no idea what you want to do next. Exercise this line of effort when you lack both imagination and information about what's out there. Discovery networking is an effective approach to uncover the unknowns. It requires curiosity and an open mindset with an intent on learning different industries, positions, and roles.

Begin by letting people know what you are interested to learn more about. Your objective is to talk to someone you already know who can share their experience about a particular industry, organization, or role. If what they are doing doesn't spark your interest, see if they'd be willing to introduce you to some of the people they know. This is how you expand your network beyond who you know to include the people they know.

During discovery networking, ask open ended questions about their experience (you can use the questions you developed based on your ideal job description). At this point, you just want to learn about what is out there. Get them talking about their experience. Focus on the relationship. Unless they ask for it, don't push your resume. If someone is giving you their time, don't burden them with the task of distributing your resume. Don't ask them where they think you might fit or what you should do. These are questions that you must answer for yourself. Your job at this point is to listen and learn.

Be gracious. This means that you should thank them for their time at the end of the conversation AND send a note expressing your gratitude. Additionally — and this holds true for all networking conversations — ask permission to keep the lines of communication open. See if they are okay with a follow up conversation in the near future. Keep all networking nodes active because it could prove beneficial later.

Once you get some clarity about the kind of organization, role, or industry that you are looking for, you can shift from discovery networking into a more informational approach. Prioritize this line of effort when you have specific questions that you are trying to answer. Some examples might include preferred credentials, transferability of skills, the hiring process, best practices for career advancement, typical career progression, benefits packages, etc. This is a personal form of intelligence collection to address your information requirements to drive decisions about potential job opportunities.

Ensure that you ask the right questions to the appropriate audience. You wouldn't ask an army infantry officer what it takes to be a pilot in the navy, so don't ask middle managers about the company's executive hiring process. If you want to know about culture, engage the general population of employees. If you want to know about strategy and vision, talk to the leaders. If you want to know about the hiring process, speak with human resources. Don't waste your time or someone else's by asking questions to people who lack the authority or experience to provide valid answers.

Along these lines, it is important to recognize that many recruiters and military hiring events are not necessarily the best resources or venues for more senior leaders or retirees. Career fairs not focused on your desired level of employment could end up being a disappointing waste of your time. Networking can be exhausting. Be deliberate with your time and energy.

The goal of every networking conversation is to get to the next conversation. That could be another networking call, a job interview, or an offer of employment. Consider statements like "look up our positions on the website," "apply online," or "give me your resume and I will get to the right person" the kiss of death. You will likely never hear from that person or company again. When you stop talking to real people you've reached the end of the line. Your choices are to reconnect with someone you had spoken to previously or move on.

The shift from informational to interview networking is often more subtle than what you might anticipate from a formal job interview. Any conversation you have that involves the people in an organization where you may work now or in the future should be considered an interview. This means that everything you do and say is on the record. Expect that hiring authorities, senior management, colleagues, and prospective employees will share notes. It is common for organizations to socialize potential hires with different business units and levels of leadership to ensure they are a good fit.

Be professional in these engagements, but also be yourself. These are people you might be spending a lot of time with, so if you don't get along, you'd probably want to know that sooner rather than later. Approach any social events the same way that you would in the military — you want to have a good time, but always be professional and respectful. Once you are invited to dinner, a sporting event, or out for drinks, you are a serious candidate under serious consideration, so take it seriously.

The timing for these networking lines of effort don't necessarily conform to traditional hiring timelines. In most cases, private organizations are looking to hire new employees between one and two months before the desired start date for the position. This is not always the case for senior leadership and executive level opportunities. If an organization anticipates a leadership vacancy, they may begin looking informally for the right backfill months in advance. Many senior leadership positions you find advertised online are often posted with a candidate already in mind. This applies primarily for corporate and private sector opportunities. If you begin pursuing a position based on what you see on the company website, there is a good chance that you're already too late. The objective of networking through these lines of effort is to set the conditions so that YOU are the person in mind for that position well before the job is posted.

False Flags

The vast majority of people you encounter in the transition space are on your side. They want you to succeed. They appreciate your service, your sacrifice, and they truly want to help. That said, there are those who feel threatened by you, and others who speak as advocates on your behalf even though they are completely unqualified to do so.

I've seen enough in this space to admit that not everyone is your ally. Even more disappointing is the fact that this happens to be true of many veterans. These are the people who appear to promote veteran employment initiatives while simultaneously marginalizing a military leader's hiring potential.

You might encounter veterans who separated after their initial term of service and have been working in the civilian sector for several years. They've paid their dues and feel threatened by the prospect of a transitioning military leader jumping the line ahead of them for more lucrative or meaningful opportunities. Some nonveterans might feel intimidated by the scope and depth of your experience. You have years and sometimes decades of education, development, and exposure to leadership challenges in extremely difficult and dynamic situations. Generally speaking, they do not. They may want you to succeed, but not if they perceive you to be a threat to their future career potential.

Because veterans are a shrinking minority of the workforce population, many employers mistakenly consider anyone who served to be an expert about any other veteran's hiring potential. I've seen veterans who departed military service before 9/11 incorrectly talk about the capabilities of those who served post-9/11. I've also seen veterans who never served in command select positions act as an authority for assessing the transferability of command leadership in the military to executive level leadership in the corporate world. In just about every case, people who have never had these experiences or held these positions will (either intentionally or unintentionally) marginalize the potential of those who have.

There is a simple solution to this problem. The limit of advance for any veteran is the limit of their own experience. If they haven't served in special operations, they can't speak to what it means to lead in the special operations community. If they haven't commanded a brigade, they cannot speak to what it takes to succeed in that level of leadership. Unfortunately, this doesn't stop many from assessing and ultimately marginalizing the potential of senior military leaders. These are the people operating in the transition space under a false flag.

You can recognize false flags by language and tone. These disingenuous advocates typically frame the conversation from the perspective of what veteran leaders cannot do. They highlight perceived gaps and dismiss the value of their experience as incompatible. Some of the more common arguments I have heard is that "senior leaders don't know business," "you don't understand profit and loss," or "you can't treat people in the civilian world the way you treat people in the military." Nobody is going to hire you for something you can't do, which is one of the reasons people operating under a false flag focus on perceived gaps and functional deficiencies.

Let's think about these arguments rationally. You've had an entire career of walking into and mastering jobs you've never done before. Despite your record of success, the prevailing opinion from these "champions" of veteran employment is that you would fail if asked to do something similar in the civilian world. That logic doesn't follow. While you may not have specific experience in a particular business or industry, your expertise is understanding people and process — two things universal to the operation of any business.

I make this argument based on my experiences as an aviation officer and battalion level commander in the army. I never flew an AH64 attack helicopter or a CH47 Chinook, but I was still responsible for approving their missions and directing their operations in combat. I have never turned a wrench on an aircraft, but I reviewed and approved all critical maintenance recovery actions (called "one-time flight approvals"). I didn't need to have the functional or technical expertise, but I did need to forge trusting relationships with those who did. A high performance team isn't one where the leader is expected to have all the answers, but rather one where leaders leverage expertise from the team to provide the best answers.

Perhaps the most egregious example of a false flag is when veterans and nonveterans alike contend that you can't put a military leader in charge of a civilian company solely because you wouldn't put a civilian leader in charge of a military unit. This assumes an analogous comparison between executive level leadership in the civilian world and command leadership in the military. This is absolutely not the case. Leader development in the military is entirely different from that in the corporate world. The military purposefully assigns you to unfamiliar positions and uncomfortable situations to develop your identity as a leader. Leader identity, the ability to show up in any situation and lead, is the core objective of the development experience in the military.

That is not the case in the civilian world. Here, functional expertise takes precedence. The best engineers become engineering managers. The engineering manager who achieves the best results is promoted to the next level. In the military, promotions are accompanied with professional military education for further leadership development. There is no comparable program to develop leader potential in the civilian world.

In the military, leader potential is the center of gravity for performance evaluation and promotion. In the civilian world, leadership is an inferred quality based on business outcomes. Comparing the leadership journey of military leaders to those in commensurate positions of authority in the civilian world — in the words of Jules Winnfield from the movie *Pulp Fiction* — "ain't the same ballpark, ain't the same league, ain't even the same damn sport." Because a service member would never consider placing a civilian leader in charge of the lives of men and women in combat without the same rigor of education and development that occurs in the military, this becomes a convenient excuse to derail the post-military potential of senior leaders.

Another example of language that contributes to the hiring bias against exceptional military leaders is labeling leadership as a "soft" skill. If you've ever been in one of these senior command or related leadership positions in your career, you know that there is nothing "soft" about them — particularly in combat. Leadership is the hardest thing you've ever done, but because there isn't an equation that directly measures the dollars and cents in a business context, it becomes a "soft" skill.

A more accurate designation would be to consider leadership a "critical" skill. People are at the core of every organizational challenge in the modern world. One of the lessons we've learned in the aftermath of COVID-19 is that the promise of higher salaries isn't bringing people back to work. People want to be inspired. They want to do meaningful work. They want to be respected and appreciated for their contributions. They want to be valued. What they are looking for is leadership, and because they aren't finding it, they are leaving the workforce. Those qualities we label as "soft" end up having decisive implications on the well-being — and ultimately the bottom line — of any organization.

This doesn't mean that every leader in the military will succeed in the civilian world any more than the top candidate on the selection list will succeed in command. Betting on potential comes with risk. Some leaders will fail. That said, it is wrong to assume that military leaders will fail simply because they lack functional business experience. Sometimes the organization is the wrong fit. Sometimes the role itself is not what the leader was looking for. What I can tell you based on the experiences of working with more than 650 senior leaders across different branches of the military and special operations community is that when given the chance, the vast majority of these leaders excel when placed into nonmilitary c-suite, executive level, and other commensurate positions of authority and responsibility.

Transition is hard enough already. It is not made any easier by veterans and nonveterans operating under a false flag. Pay attention to the language and tone of your conversations. Listen when it is honest and empowering. Walk away if it is dismissive and limiting. Focus on what you *can* do instead of what you *can't* do. The transition into any civilian position of authority will be difficult. That doesn't mean that you are unqualified for these positions any more than you were unqualified for every unfamiliar position you were assigned in the military.

Credentialing Constraints

The lack of understanding and familiarity about military service perpetuates an overwhelming impulse to validate the skills and experience of military leaders. Credentials — like the very popular Project Management Professional (PMP) — can be extremely beneficial. However, the strength of your value proposition comes from the knowledge and wisdom of your experience — not a piece of paper. Sometimes a credential can become a constraint.

Let's explore how this happens in more detail using the PMP certification. Most junior leaders meet the standards for the PMP early in their professional careers. In the first five to ten years, you've met all the requirements for this credential. If you served in the military longer than that, you have other experiences — beyond the PMP — that contribute to your value proposition. If you allow this credential to become the core of your value proposition — prominently displayed in the subheading of your LinkedIn profile, you are vastly underselling yourself. You are stepping back to a level of competence you mastered much earlier in your career.

Once you are promoted to the rank of colonel in the army, you probably wouldn't find captain level work fulfilling. You've already done that. Yes, you are qualified for that kind of work, but you have so much more to offer. Furthermore, the discerning employer knows that if they hired you into that kind of role, you won't stay long. You will get bored and eventually leave for something else.

This can be very frustrating as you watch employers pursue the candidates with a fraction of your education and experience. Don't take it personally. In most cases, those recruiters are not looking for senior level leaders. They are looking to hire project managers — not leaders of project managers. Senior level positions are less prevalent and harder to come by.

If you brand yourself by a certification, then you significantly increase the chance that you will get hired based on that specific qualification or skill. Don't allow a credential to become a constraint. If you don't have more confidence in your potential beyond a specific credential, employers won't either. Before you invest the time and effort, understand how any certification will further your hiring potential based on the totality of your value proposition.

Personal Branding

Let's demystify the narrative. It isn't a sales pitch. For any position of significance, an employer isn't going to hire you based on what you say in the first 45 seconds of a conversation. Think about it — would you really want to work for someone who makes decisions like that when there is no urgency to do so? Probably not. Here's something else to think about: If they could hire you on a whim, they could probably fire you just as easily. Hiring leaders for any organization is a process, and your narrative is only a small part of that process.

This is not to say that telling your story isn't important. Used appropriately, a narrative can authentically connect with your audience on an emotional level. That emotional connection is how you are remembered after the conversation. Based on the nature of our open limbic system, that connection begins when you first walk into the room.

Because of the mirror neurons in our prefrontal cortex, we not only sense but also imitate the emotions of the people around us in only a fraction of a second. This allows us to rapidly sense and react to potential threats. In nonthreatening situations, it allows us to recognize and understand the emotions of others to satisfy our social and biological imperative for connection. Consequently, the best way to ensure that someone has a certain impression about you when they walk out of the room is for you to bring that emotion with you as your walking into the room.

It is understandable if you find the entire networking and interview process unsettling. As military leaders, we come from a culture of forced humility. We are expected to accept responsibility when things go poorly and champion the team when things go well. This feeds our imposter syndrome, the belief that we are not good enough despite the vast evidence of success throughout our careers. Because others subconsciously feed off your emotions, it becomes extremely difficult to convey a positive impression when you are consumed by fear or anxiety at the prospect of talking about yourself.

Owning your story and priming are two strategies that can help you overcome this challenge. Owning your story means anchoring your dialogue in the facts. You have a documented record of performance in your assignment history, evaluation reports, and award citations. If it is written in black and white, think of it as a verifiable fact. Owning your story is a form of reporting what's already been documented about you.

Focusing on the facts of your story can also safeguard you from broadcasting any insecurity. There is a difference between being authentic and being arrogant. Authenticity is being who you are and owning the achievements of your career. Arrogance emerges when you compare yourself to others. Whenever you compare yourself to people who are not present, the person you are talking to becomes the object of your comparison. For example, if you talk about how you "turn failing organizations around," "transform toxic cultures," or "fix what's broken," what are you implying about your audience's organization? Are you seeking a leadership role because you believe their organization is failing? These comparisons are a form of insecurity — the ability to prop yourself up by pushing others down. If you believed in your abilities, you wouldn't need to anchor your value from such a negative foundation. The negativity from this type of arrogance carries a lot of weight in a conversation, and all that negativity clings to you. Because people are inclined to remember the negative, this insecurity becomes a liability.

Another technique to prepare yourself for interviews is through priming. You are probably already familiar with the practice of positive visualization — conducting a mental rehearsal of a specific task or action before performing that task or action. Athletes see themselves run the route, hit the ball, or make the shot before they enter the game. Priming is a related construct that focuses on emotional preparation.

Priming is an application of Dr. Barbara Fredrickson's Broaden and Build Theory from positive psychology. It is a mindfulness practice that involves reflecting on an event or activity when you experienced the positive emotions that you want to bring to a situation. For example, if you want to be excited, you reflect on a memory where you were extremely excited. If you want to be confident, you reflect on a time when you were most confident. Researchers found that by thinking about the feeling, you actually create that feeling.

Priming has real implications on performance. Researchers worked with doctors tasked to make a difficult prognosis, sales people about to close a tough sale, and high achieving math students who were about to take a challenging test. One population went through a priming exercise, while the other population went through their normal preparation routine. The results of these studies showed that the primed population significantly outperformed the control group.

Priming works on a neurological level. When we face an uncertain or potentially challenging situation, we have an immediate, subconscious fight-or-flight reaction. Our survival mechanism attempts to protect us. The release of certain hormones increases blood flow in some areas of the brain while decreasing it in others. Our pupils dilate, heart rate increases, and our attention becomes more acute. Other functions, however, are intentionally degraded because the brain assumes these functions are a lesser priority. If you've ever had a mental block and could not recall specific details or noticed that nobody seems to be listening during a shouting argument, you bore witness to the impaired brain functions that include access to long term memory, empathy, and active listening as a result of this phenomenon.

Once fear or anxiety shut down these parts of the brain, they become difficult to open up again. The voice inside your head begins to ruminate in ways that further reinforce this reaction. Through priming, you essentially bypass this switch and open the circuit from the other side of your brain. Emotion feeds the thought instead of the thought feeding the emotion. As a consequence, the doctor can be more creative in linking their learning and experience to make an accurate prognosis. The sales representative can make meaningful connections to close the sale. The math student can dip into their long term memory to find solutions.

Once you are in the right place emotionally, we can focus on what you want to say. The objective is to connect to your audience by summarizing your life in less than a minute. This is not the time to push your resume. If you are looking for any position of responsibility, chances are that your audience has already reviewed your resume or LinkedIn profile. If they haven't, you can bet they will soon after this conversation. Personal and vulnerable details are more impactful and memorable than any of the impressive details from your career. In the words of Maya Angelou, people remember how you made them feel, not what you say.

One way to frame the narrative is to break it down into three parts. The first part is the introduction. Make it personal and relatable. Talking about leading small and large teams isn't very interesting (or impressive) and likely something your audience will already know. A potential place to begin is the reason why you joined the military. Everyone who graduates high school has to make initial choices about the path they take into adulthood, so you can start there:

I didn't want to just go to college after high school. My family couldn't afford it, and I wanted to do something exciting. I didn't know anything about the military, but I applied to West Point because it was free and different from the regular college experience. Two weeks after my high school graduation, I became a cadet and began my journey through the army.

Personal details are both unique and relatable. That is what makes them memorable. They distinguish your journey from every other leader from the military.

Once you've made a genuine introduction, sum up your career using language that doesn't require a security clearance or military experience:

I became a pilot in the army because I wanted to fly, but I stayed and made it a career because of the people. I have been successful as a leader in the army because I see uncomfortable situations as opportunities to grow, I lead by inspiring others to achieve high performance outcomes, and I leverage creativity and a drive for innovation to solve the most difficult problems.

When you summarize the things you did well, you are guiding the future direction of the conversation. In this example, you might notice that there aren't any numbers or references to military units. Numbers are processed in different parts of the brain from where we process and experience emotions. If you regurgitate numbers and acronyms, your conversation becomes harder to follow. On a subconscious level, your listener is not with you. They are too busy bouncing from one side of their brain to the other to make sense of what you are saying.

Finish the conversation by sharing what you are passionate about pursuing in life beyond the military. Any organization looking for senior or executive level leaders will want to know that anyway:

I am passionate about coaching and personal development to bridge the gap between confidence and potential. I want to inspire leaders and teams to achieve more than they thought possible.

Leave your audience excited about what excites you using emotive language.

Once you've outlined your narrative, try it out on people who really know you — like your spouse or a close friend. Ask them if what you are saying sounds like you, and if not, then ask about what is missing. Ask them how they feel after they've heard your narrative and compare that to the impression you hope to leave at the conclusion of the conversation. The feeling is how you will be remembered, and how you make people feel defines your personal brand.

Telling Stories that Matter

By the time you sit down for an interview, the organization already knows you're qualified. They wouldn't be wasting their time otherwise. An interview is a chance to tell your story — in a way that connects your value proposition to the requirements of a particular opportunity.

To put it bluntly, the organization wants to know if you are the right fit. This is as much about personality as it is about qualifications. Authenticity matters. The two most important things you could do in an interview is be yourself and be positive.

There are a number of templates for telling stories that matter to your audience. One popular template is the Situation, Task, Action, and Result or STAR Format. This helps to focus on the relevant details. When military leaders talk about our experiences, we tend to focus on the context of the situation and the problem. Based on our own experience, we already know what actions were necessary to achieve the mission. We don't go into details about our actions (how you contributed) or the results (what you achieved). We talk in terms of where and when we did the work and less about how we did it or what we achieved.

Unfortunately, when you are talking to someone outside the military, those overlooked details are the ones that matter. A potential employer cares more about how you were able to do something — the actions you took as a leader — and the specifics of what you achieved. They want to understand how your results contributed to the bigger picture. They are trying to connect those actions and results to the specifics of a job requirement and what their organization wants to achieve.

How you tell the story is critical. Relevance is more important than the "wow" factor. I could share with you some exciting stories about flying MEDEVAC missions in Afghanistan. I could describe coming over the mountain, diving the aircraft into the cover of the trees, taking fire along the way, and pulling casualties out of an active firefight. That is an exhilarating story that has nothing to do with most opportunities in the business sector.

Alternatively, I can talk about the same event from an entirely different perspective — one that resonates with what an employer might need. I can explain how we built trust and trained our team to excel in high pressure situations. I could discuss how we managed talent and leveraged strengths

77

across the unit to create team synergy and offset risk. I can share how we optimized processes and encouraged creative thinking to find innovative ways to get an aircraft off the ground in less time than prescribed by the operator manual. I could also talk about how we collaborated with more than a dozen military, civilian, and international agencies scattered throughout Afghanistan to streamline a complex approval process down to a few minutes. This is a totally different story about the exact same event, but one that may better connect with what is relevant to a future employer.

Make it easy for your audience to recognize your value. Stories about you should matter to your audience. Craft your stories in a way that the actions and results speak directly to their needs. Your objective is not to impress them with your record of past service but to impress upon them how you can deliver and contribute to their objectives moving forward. I am certain they will be grateful for your service, but you want them walking away from the interview with the confidence that you have what it takes to make meaningful contributions to their team.

The True Meaning of Loyalty

We value loyalty. Our loyalty runs so deep that we are willing to sacrifice our very lives for our unit, our mission, and our nation. We make this commitment out of a sense of pride and with the comfort that comes from belonging to something greater than ourselves. The true meaning of loyalty to the mission as you enter the transition process and embark upon future job opportunities means being loyal to yourself.

We believe that we matter. As military leaders, we are important people with important responsibilities. People count on us. If we don't put the unit before everything else, other people will suffer. We've given far too much over our lifetime to allow the team to fail. This is why we continue to show up early and stay late even when we should be focusing on our transition. Thinking about your needs is selfish — and a little bit scary. It is far easier and more comfortable to go into the breach once more with our dear friends. We cope with stress by pouring ourselves into our work. This is what we do because it is what we have always done.

Get used to the idea that the unit will be just fine after you leave. Everyone who volunteers for the service will inevitably leave the service, and the military — as the army song suggests — keeps rolling along. There is a fine line between loyalty to the unit and a level of self-importance that borders on narcissism. This is where you need some measure of humility. Others can pick up your mantle and continue the mission in the same way that you picked it up from those before you.

In some cases, fear of leaving creates a codependency that hides behind the mask of loyalty. We believe the unit needs us when actually it is we who need the unit. Others across the military may also experience this fear as they approach the threshold of transition. Here is an opportunity to redirect your courage and truly lean into the process as a positive example for them. Living the example for transitioning well is the final and perhaps most important contribution you will make as a military leader.

It is also worth noting that loyalty in the civilian world has a different meaning. Our general orders tell us to perform our duties to the limit of our ability until properly relieved. If you happen to not like your job — tough. Perform your duties. You swore an oath. You serve at the pleasure and needs of the institution. That is your obligation. Loyalty to your oath, the mission, and the organization is everything.

Employers in the corporate world aren't operating under the same constraints. There are no restrictions on possible candidates to fill a role. If nobody wants the job, they can offer better compensation to attract better candidates. You can't do that in the military. Civilian employers don't have the authority to assign someone into a specific role against their will. If you accept a role and decide that job isn't for you, you can leave. You don't have to wait for the next PCS cycle. It might be inconvenient for the employer, but rest assured, they will find someone else.

Here is where we need to have some humility as it applies to the civilian job market. You might be very capable for a particular job, but if you don't want to do that work, then you are probably not the best candidate for that role. This is a consideration that doesn't apply in the military. Even when you accept an employment offer, you have the right to change your mind. What is best for you and your family has a tendency to change. Life happens. This could be based on what you learn through the process, your personal circumstances, or even a more lucrative offer. For whatever the reason, if the job is not the best fit for you, then you are not doing yourself or the organization any favor by staying in the job. You are just preventing the organization from finding a better candidate — one who is both capable and willing to fill that role.

Think about this from the employer's perspective. You want a capable, well-qualified candidate. Given the choice, you also want someone who is passionate about the work and committed to the organization. This is particularly true for leadership positions. You want inspired leaders on your team. So, if you are not inspired or fully committed, the best way to demonstrate loyalty to that organization is to get out of the way and let them find another capable, well-qualified candidate who is.

Loyalty requires both humility and honesty. Humility to recognize that you are not the be all and end all for a specific position. In the military, someone will replace you when you leave. In the civilian world, someone else might be better suited for that position. Honesty is admitting that doing what is best for you is also what is best for the employer. Humility and honesty are best for the military unit you are leaving and the civilian workforce you are entering. The combination of these qualities reveal the true meaning of loyalty as you embark upon your transition from military service.

THE ARRIVAL HOME

I *had a rocky start to the rehabilitation process. Every day started with a blood pressure reading and the hookup — placing cardiac leads on my chest and abdomen so that technicians could monitor my heart during physical activity. Every Tuesday and Thursday for nine weeks I would begin my four hour rehabilitation session on the treadmill.*

I couldn't do much in the beginning. I had a persistent arrhythmia and my ejection fraction (EF) — the measure of how much blood was being pumped from the left ventricle of the heart, was only 40 percent. The low end of a healthy EF was around 50 percent. I started my physical therapy walking at a slow pace for about 20 minutes. At periodic intervals, a nurse would record my heart rate and blood pressure.

After the exercise portion of the session, there were a series of group meetings. The first was about mindfulness and relaxation, the second was a form of group therapy for emotional wellness, and the final one was about nutrition and education about heart health.

My cohort included other patients from the hospital network across the Jacksonville area. With one exception, I was the youngest person in my cohort. Most of the participants were my parents' age. If you looked at a group photo of my cohort, I was the clear outlier. That said, I also had the most serious heart condition. Most of the people in the program were there to prevent a cardiac event. I already had one, and a significant one at that. As is the case with most veterans, you can't just look at them to determine how healthy they are.

I had a significant scare during the second week of the program. I was on the exercise bike. On the other side of the room was an elderly gentleman on an ergonomic bicycle. We were facing each other. We were only about 20 feet apart, so you couldn't help but watch each other work out. I wasn't a fan of cycling, and I liked stationary bikes even less. I was peddling quite hard to get to my target heart rate, and he was moving slowly . . . very slowly.

About 15 minutes into the exercise session, he started to slump and fall off the machine. He collapsed. The nurse ran over to him, but couldn't get to him through the maze of equipment. I jumped off the stationary bike and ran over to him. The staff couldn't move the equipment, so I did. The soldier in me kicked in and I completely ignored the fact that I had no business exerting myself to move exercise equipment. I lifted the bikes and treadmills to create a path to the patient. The nurse used a defibrillator while I and another gentleman performed chest compressions at her guidance. The remaining staff marshaled our group into another room and notified the paramedics.

I cleared a path through the equipment so that the EMTs could navigate the small space. I was breathing heavily and sweating profusely. Exercise equipment is really heavy. The leads from the heart rate monitoring equipment were dangling from my body. The ambulance arrived within 20 minutes. A person whose name I can't remember was carted off to the hospital. He had a heart attack. Not the most encouraging experience when beginning a program of cardiac rehabilitation.

This happened on a Tuesday morning. On Thursday, we learned that the gentleman did not survive. He passed away at the hospital later that evening. How ironic that I would bear witness to what transpired just a month earlier along the trail outside my neighborhood. The difference being that I came back. He didn't.

Over the course of the next two months, I would integrate some new habits into my life. I started to practice mindfulness. I began to record when I experienced joy in my life. What started out as a small list grew rapidly. In the process, I became more present in those moments that mattered most to me. I would return to therapy to help process my experiences in Afghanistan. Although I didn't incorporate all of the dietary recommendations through the program, I made significant changes to my eating habits.

The simple fact is that I am not the same person who joined the military a month after my 18th birthday. I am not the same person who deployed to combat the first, second, or third time. I am not the same person who retired out of battalion command. These are the chapters from my past — my odyssey — that I have shared with you. You also have a story that deserves to be told — the story of your journey. Some parts are exciting, some parts are scary, and there are probably even some parts you'd rather forget, but the good, the bad, and even the ugly are all part of your odyssey. At the end of it, you won't be the same. Different can be better. YOU can be better. You can become something more and return home as the hero of your own story.

I completed cardiac rehabilitation a week before Christmas. My EF had risen to 60 percent, well into the healthy range. My blood pressure was normal. I felt great. On the last day of the program, I decided to go for a run on the treadmill. I didn't require any monitoring equipment. I wanted to run a little faster for a little longer, so I did. I finished at 6.84 miles, just beyond the distance I ran when I collapsed three months earlier. I also held a pace nearly a minute faster than I did on that fateful day in September.

The journey home is going to be hard. There is so much to process, and it won't all make sense at first. That is okay. You are not alone. You can do this. I came back stronger. So can you. Finish better. We are waiting and counting on you here on the other side of life beyond the military. How you experience your transition is a choice. Set your intention to flourish in veteran life.

ABOUT THE AUTHOR

Jason Roncoroni is a retired Lieutenant Colonel and former aviation battalion commander from the United States Army. He served 33 months in combat and has the unique distinction of having transitioned from the military twice. He authored the bestselling book *Beyond the Military: A Leader's Handbook for Warrior Reintegration.* As the founder and president of Ordinary Hero Coaching, he continues to work with senior leaders across all services and the special operations community through their transition from military service. Jason is a Master Certified Coach (MCC) from the International Coaching Federation who specializes in Positive Psychology Coaching and integrating the practice of applied positive psychology into the coaching experience.

GRATITUDE

The Defenders of the Free (the 1993 graduating class from United States Military Academy) provided the inspiration for this book. I was disturbed to learn that suicide was the leading cause of death among my classmates, many of whom spent most of their careers serving repeated deployments to combat zones in places like Afghanistan and Iraq. I had my own experience with death as a result of my service, but I came back. I believe that miracle comes with a responsibility to help others find their way home. I am grateful to God, my extended family, and all the friends that supported my wife and children when I was fighting for my life. I want to thank them for enduring all the hardship and sacrifice from my military service. To Aidan and Everett, I hope to be a positive and loving example of leadership and service, and to my wife, Jill — I hope I can be the man worthy of your love until the end of time. For my classmates and everyone who struggles through transition — this is for you. May you find your path in life beyond the military — one with the meaning and happiness you deserve.

Jason Roncoroni
DOTF '93